Bridging Human and Machine: Future Education with Intelligence

Series Editors

Shengquan Yu, School of Educational Technology, Beijing Normal University, Beijing, China

Ig Ibert Bittencourt, Computing Institute, Federal University of Alagoas, Maceió, Brazil

This book series will gather researchers from AI to brain science, scientists from data science to cognitive neuroscience; experts from academia to industry, and specifically pay attentions on the new frontiers and technologies that would transform future education. This series intends to empower readers a deeper understanding on future education from the perspectives of both enabling technology and learning science. Topics are covered but not limited to the cutting-edge and multidisciplinary research, development, and practice among the fields in education and technology. For example, some books would address what and how AI techniques can be used for enhancing learning and education system. Some books would seek an explanation on how brain science can connect human brain's physical activities and cognitive process. Moreover, this book series would provide policy-makers and educational stakeholders more quality and equity education, and encourage government and private sectors to invest more resources in the development of educational tools and facilities with intelligence.

Fatima Roumate
Editor

Artificial Intelligence in Higher Education and Scientific Research

Future Development

IISR

Springer

Editor
Fatima Roumate
International Institute of Scientific Research
Marrakech, Morocco

ISSN 2662-5342 ISSN 2662-5350 (electronic)
Bridging Human and Machine: Future Education with Intelligence
ISBN 978-981-19-8640-6 ISBN 978-981-19-8641-3 (eBook)
https://doi.org/10.1007/978-981-19-8641-3

This Springer imprint is published by the registered company Springer Nature Singapore Pte Ltd.
The registered company address is: 152 Beach Road, #21-01/04 Gateway East, Singapore 189721, Singapore

Foreword

As I write this foreword at the beginning of the third decade of the third millennium, humanity is experiencing severe system disruptions. Much ink has been spilled on the crisis-level situations in the area of planetary ecosystems, health systems, and the impact of technology on society. We need to spend more time looking at disruptions in education systems as well.

There is no escape from the direct impact of all these changes on our individual and societal well-being.

UNESCO's Information for All Programme has the mandate to encourage policies that promote equitable and equitable approaches to our digitally mediated future. It, therefore, encourages evidence-based policy based on research and practice. This book can be seen as one of the building blocks toward that goal. The chapters range in focus from the transformation of institutions of higher learning to the fundamental changes that are taking place at the level of neuroscience that affect our approach to learning.

The field of higher education and scientific research is central to our preparedness and eventual strategies for dealing with the transformative changes that are currently being experienced. At the same time, the higher education sector is itself in the process of a rapid and far-reaching transition. Much of this change is directly linked to the increased use of tools based on artificial intelligence.

We observe increased use of blended learning, integration of social media, greater dependency on the use of audio-visual supports, and deliberate integration of findings from cognitive neuroscience in how EdTech and teacher–researchers design and deliver content as well as in how they monitor individual learners. In turn, these developments have a significant impact on the nature of business models used in the sector and the multiplicity of EdTech players. The increasing footprint of platform companies introduces new concerns in terms of power asymmetries as well as language, values, and cultural dominance. On another level entirely, we observe that there are relatively few institutions equipped to conduct advanced research in artificial intelligence as the huge data sets necessary for some research are concentrated in the hands of relatively few institutions in just a few countries.

These issues are addressed in this timely collection of chapters. For example, one chapter explores the use of artificial intelligence in research and how it affects human volition and bias in interpretation and ultimately encourages plagiarism creating new roles for advisors if science and innovation are to be socially sustainable. Another predicts the death of the university as we know it today. This same chapter explores the changes taking place at the professional level for professors and researchers and explores their interaction with new technologies. The exploration of ways in which new technologies are changing approaches to teaching, learning, and research which are common themes in several chapters. One of the chapters explores this situation in-depth using some case studies with a focus on educational sovereignty. It looks at the use of foreign languages and the intensive use of foreign EdTech by teachers and learners. It also explores the implications of the absence of national cloud infrastructure for safeguarding the data of learners and for digital sovereignty as a whole.

The critical dimensions of neuroscience and neurotechnology and the manipulation of the electrical activity of the brain, sometimes called neuro-hacking, are addressed in two important papers. More educators need to become aware of these issues and the implications for their work. It is a field that reminds us of the importance of the work done by UNESCO in developing the Recommendation of the Ethics of Artificial Intelligence adopted by the Member States in 2021. More educators need to engage around these topics, and Governments need to develop clear policies. It is alarming that in some quarters there is a perception that the complexity of these challenges makes it difficult to change our trajectory. We can and must act if we are to successfully achieve the sustainable development goals.

While this book of proceedings provides us with some interesting insights into the current situation, it should be seen as a catalyst for further research. I encourage readers to take the work presented here to the next level and to continue to explore these issues in their country's contexts while continuing to engage at a global level to shape the balance of the millennium.

Paris, France

Dorothy Gordon
Chair, UNESCO Information for All Programme

Introduction

The theme of this volume highlights two central domains where artificial intelligence (AI) offers new possibilities and imposes new challenges to higher education and scientific research. AI has facilitated the exchange of instantaneous, universal, and multidirectional information. The global impact of AI in these domains has sparked heated debates among scholars, legal, professionals, governments, entrepreneurs, and many other actors. Universities, as producers of knowledge, occupy a central place in these debates. Understanding the current and future impact of AI on higher education and scientific research is thus a critical and timely task. AI technologies provide free and easy access to information and big data. It connects people and ensures access to education for all. In this way, AI has fundamentally affected the methods and the culture of teaching and learning in many of today's societies, and the changes are spreading to every corner of the world.

How AI is influencing higher education and scientific research? and how this field will help to enhance a positive impact and reduce the AI-generated risks imposed by AI?

What is the role of higher education in the societal and economic changes created by AI? Are universities prepared to respond and support these changes? Is higher education able to prepare students for the challenges posed by AI as they enter the workforce and become our future leaders? What opportunities and challenges do universities face? What are the short-term and long-term benefits and costs of using AI in higher education? Could ethics on AI help to face all-new challenges imposed by AI?

These questions and others will be discussed in this edited book. As AI rapidly develops, its momentum in society as a whole and its use in higher education and scientific research create an urgent need for scholarly inquiry. The application of AI in higher education can bring about immediate and positive outcomes in sustainable development. Changes that could affect societies on a grand scale calls for all players (governments, universities, and the private sector) to devise strategies that will maximize positive results.

In this volume, we provide a rich range of analyses of AI as a tool used in higher education and scientific research, which contributes to their interaction. The key focus is the interaction between AI and higher education and scientific research. On the one hand, AI has a role in facilitating higher education and science. On the other hand, research and scientific creativity, and innovation will further enhance the development of AI.

In Chap. 1, Monte-Serrat and Cattani discussed education as a function of State Apparatus from a point of view of Althusser's theory (2012, p. 80). They introduced new professional functions to the professor called according to the authors of this chapter, "advisor/professor" and "guide-professor" who should ensure mediation between States and researchers and create the balance in the "relationship between States, educational organ and society". This new function of the guiding professor leads us, according to Monte-Serrat and Cattani, to make science and innovation socially sustainable through a combination of research and AI considering their views both on scientific research and AI ethics.

AI and COVID-19 or what Marius Vacarelu, called in Chap. 2 of this volume technological—medical transformation increase the importance of the relationship between higher education systems and States. According to the author (op. cit), the reinforcement of the relationship between States or political environment and actors in the higher education system is important in the age of AI considering the importance of the balance between legal rules and ethics of AI to face current and future challenges imposed by AI. For Marius Vacarelu, Parliaments need to produce new legal mechanisms related to AI's impact on higher education. Likewise, researchers should suggest solutions to all legal challenges related to AI that legislators will face in the future, considering new roles in higher education and scientific research in the era of AI. It concerns several changes both in informational and in financial dimensions as it is discussed by Meriem Rafik in her chapter. She argued that it is necessary to manage what she called "the job of scientific influencer" to avoid misinformation and that higher education is unique in its power to catalyze social and economic changes, and this power will be enhanced in the future considering trends of AI-related to this sector. This lead us to the rise of the hybrid system and the difference between traditional and virtual universities as was discussed by Karim Hamidouch in Chap. 4. Focusing on how COVID-19 accelerated the transition from "traditional" universities to the hybrid system, he underlined that the future of education will be multiple. In a sense, Olga V. Novoselova discussed in Chap. 5, the modern forms of virtual internationalization and the expansion of flexible distance provision, continue to be powerful trends during the pandemic COVID-19. This pandemic was characterized by the evolution of more strategic approaches elaborated by universities to face the virtual competitiveness related to the pandemic and AI technologies. According to the author (op. cit), the expansion of virtual mobility and E-universities is another trend related to AI and the pandemic. This trend requires new strategies and policy actions with special attention to AI infrastructures and governance. The goal is to ensure sustainable development for society considering all the transformations related to the use of AI in higher education. This argument is explained by Viktor Zinchenko, the author of Chap. 6. This dimension is important when all actors are impressed by AI's impacts on higher education and scientific research. According to the author of this chapter, researchers, and programmers, in Chap. 5, all actors should decide together on the degree of AI use in higher education. New strategies and policy actions are an obligation rather than a choice considering biases and malicious uses of AI on higher education and scientific research and the growing number of global cybercrime damage according to Fatima Roumate, the author of the last chapter titled "Ethics of AI, Higher Education and Scientific Research". The author presents choking statistics of cyberattacks in higher education. Several universities are taking cybersecurity to the top and are dedicated an important budget to making their platforms secure. International instruments and regional initiatives on the ethics of AI are the only way to ensure the protection of students and teachers. Ethics are the only way to create the counterbalance between rules and algorithms as was argued by Fatima Roumate.

This collection of articles offers us a rich variety of pertinent analyses and case studies where the relations between AI and higher education and scientific research are addressed in very interesting and multiple ways. The multidisciplinary approach offers a large umbrella of issues related to the subject of this volume. In the age of AI and considering technological sovereignty, but more the changing identity of international society and societies, new strategies at international, regional and national levels are crucial. This volume is a call for action.

Fatima Roumate
President of the International
Institute of Scientific Research
Marrakech, Morocco

Reference

Althusser, L. (2012). Ideology and ideological state apparatuses (Notes towards an investigation). *Media and Cultural Studies: Keyworks, 80.*

Contents

Chapter 1
Artificial Intelligence and Scientific Research: Values at Stake in Education

Dioneia Motta Monte-Serrat and Carlo Cattani

Abstract Education is associated with the political responsibility of specialized institutions, whose representative, as a research advisor, is assigned the function of mediating positive and negative aspects of the use of artificial intelligence by appreciating the values at stake. Artificial intelligence, AI, is associated with the debate about its effects on volition: While, in research, human choice is aided by a creative mind that appreciates the context of reality, AI offers 'ready-to-use' elements, large volume and sometimes out of context, favoring bias in interpretation and enhancing the practice of plagiarism. These are negative aspects that 'petrify' the research content. We explain that the advisor has a mediating role when examining situations that require efficiency and productivity as opposed to the need for experience and creativity in scientific research. This role of mediator makes the advisor fit perfectly into the concept of education as a dynamic process, keeping the research activity from inattentive 'consumption' of the information provided by AI, which can hinder creativity in research or make it converge to idealized preferences (bias). In this way, the advisor combines research and artificial intelligence, weighing principles and values at stake that cannot be forgotten in education and stimulating opportunities for science and innovation to be socially sustainable.

Keywords Education · Artificial intelligence · Scientific research · Mediation · Creativity

---

D. M. Monte-Serrat (✉)
Computation and Mathematics Department, University of Sao Paulo, Rua Rui Barbosa, 599, ap 121, Ribeirao Preto, SP 14015-120, Brazil
e-mail: di_motta61@yahoo.com.br; deserrat@unaerp.br

Law Department, University of Ribeirao Preto, Rua Rui Barbosa, 599, ap 121, Ribeirao Preto, SP 14015-120, Brazil

C. Cattani
Mathematical Physics and Applied Mathematics at the Engineering School, Tuscia University, Via del Paradiso, 47, 01100 Viterbo, Italy
e-mail: cattani@unitus.it

F. Roumate (ed.), *Artificial Intelligence in Higher Education and Scientific Research*, Bridging Human and Machine: Future Education with Intelligence,
https://doi.org/10.1007/978-981-19-8641-3_1

1.1 Introduction

Facilitation of learning, teaching, and research is essential to the formation of citizens, and, for this reason, it is ensured by the Universal Declaration of Human Rights (1948, art. 26). The task of educating and shaping objectives, forms, processes, and methods is a political responsibility (Althusser, 2012; Frankena et al., 2002).

This article articulates the values at stake in education with the use of artificial intelligence as a scientific research tool. Questions arise about how public education policies prepare new generations of researchers for what is new. There is a tendency in research to decrease the 'old way of teaching' assumed by the face-to-face mediation of an advisor professor, for the increasing adoption of knowledge through new tools of intelligent systems involving time management, instructional strategies in the development of content, and considerations on issues related to online students (Kebritchi et al., 2017; Monte-Serrat & Cattani, 2020).

The Economist's (2021) future-gazing analysis of the world in 2021 realizes that we are all subject to having more digital assistants to work efficiently; congresses or work meetings will not return to being in person as they were if they can be done online; productivity no longer depends on a guide that observes students, as it is through platforms that results and efficiency are measured; few places will retain physical structures as in the past; today's technology companies will be able to replace others that have done the same job; highly technological solutions and experiences supported with digital assistance are being valued more; everything can be copied or replicated; the workforce will be reduced and many simple operations will be provided by AI; education will not be the same; everyone is responsible for studying what they need; and schools and universities are being transformed into a hybrid scheme forever.

Although these innovations can be viewed as a new beginning, some considerations must be taken into account when it comes to education. Changes are very welcome since they do not weigh negatively on the new reality and the search for new paths. These issues are the subject of this article, and to assess what is at stake in the transmission of knowledge, we begin clarifying some aspects of education.

1.1.1 Education as the 'Longa Manus' of the State

Education, according to Althusser's theory (2012, p. 80, 2014), is a function of State Apparatus. The author (op. cit.) distinguishes between State Power, State Apparatus, and State Ideological Apparatuses, ISA. The ISAs are not to be confused with the State's repressive Apparatuses (Government, Administration, Army, Police, Courts, Prisons, etc.), which act through violence. For Althusser, ISA is a certain number of realities that are presented to the observer in the form of distinct and specialized institutions, constituting a body that is not immediately visible. Examples of State Ideological Apparatuses are the religious ISA; the educational ISA (public and private schools); the ISA family; the legal ISA; the political ISA; the ISA union; the communications ISA (press, radio, television, etc.); and the cultural ISA (Althusser, 2012, p. 80).

When talking about education, we must take into account a 'space', evidence, before it: the State (Pêcheux, 1975, pp. 147–148, 1988). It is the State, therefore, that dictates the discourse of science, better saying, the values at stake in the scientific research, carrying out this task through rules and norms elaborated by the State organ responsible for education.

For Henry (1977), the development of sciences is related to the development of schooling and this link shows the existence, in ideological superstructures, of an ideological apparatus of the State articulating sciences, theoretical ideologies, and practical ideologies, ensuring a unified form of meaning. Haroche (1984, pp. 19–20) discusses that ideologies (political, legal, religious, educational, etc.) inscribe power in certain disciplinary devices to facilitate transparency, measurability, and modifiability.

1.1.2 Mediation Between State and Researchers

Education as political responsibility makes the advisor/professor a mediator between the State and researchers. It is the responsibility of the guide professor to deliberately create possibilities for learning that aim to develop the skills of researchers, which includes the improvement of knowledge and the transmission of skills of everyday life (Belgacem et al., 2019). It is in this relationship between the State, education organs, and society that the mediation of the professional in education is found.

Education is not only an instrument for the administration of research and the researcher but it is also the possibility of opening a new dimension in the learning process of this researcher. It is with this vision that one can improve skills in education: articulating new domains for the inclusion of data provided by intelligent systems, to be managed and mediated by the education professional. In the ongoing relationship among the education professional, the researcher, and artificial intelligence, we propose the possibility of changing course in scientific research, in order not to sanitize paths and, at the same time, sustain plurality through practices implied in discovery to transform reality. It is believed that with this perspective of the relationship between scientific research and artificial intelligence, shelf studies with their cooling, silencing, and paralyzing sense are refuted (Campos & Furtado, 2011), to establish studies that transform the world, subjects, and organizations.

This article is divided into 5 sections. After introducing the concept of education and relating it to the political responsibility of distinct and specialized institutions, Sect. 1.1 addresses the positive and negative aspects of research and the use of artificial intelligence in the transmission of knowledge, giving the professor advisor the position of arbiter in charge of appreciating the values at stake. Section 1.2 deals with artificial intelligence, AI, as a tool designed for quick solutions to problems difficult to solve for humans. We debate about volition versus the use of AI, showing that the human choice is aided by a creative mind that also removes information from the context of reality; and, on the other hand, AI offers 'ready-to-use' elements in large volume and sometimes out of context, which favors the imposition of interest group perspectives (bias). We also discuss the false belief that scientific research is enhanced by the facilities of the Internet, which through easy access to text search engines increases the practice of plagiarism. We argue that these negative aspects 'petrify' the concept of research, which was expected to be new and creative. Section 1.3, in turn, examines efficiency and productivity in scientific research versus experience and creativity, showing that public policies tend to set standards as prerequisites to be achieved as targets, putting pressure on academics and researchers to look for numbers at the expense of creative content of the research. We show that experience and creativity presuppose a personal exchange between advisor and researcher, going beyond methodological rigor. The advisor professor acting as a counterbalance is the subject of Sect. 1.4. They, as representatives of the State, must comply with the scientific discourse guidelines designed under controlled conditions and, at the same time, provide opportunities for there to be a disruption of pre-established values that only reiterate findings. This mediation role of the advisor depends on the interpersonal relationship and fits perfectly into the concept of education as a dynamic process, giving it the necessary flexibility. The conclusion, in Sect. 1.5, calls attention to avoiding an inattentive 'consumption' of information provided by AI, which could hinder creativity in research, or make it converge to idealized preferences (bias). This is the function of the guide professor: combining research and artificial intelligence weighing principles and values at stake that cannot be forgotten. This is the means of educating by encouraging opportunities for science and innovation to be socially sustainable.

1.2 Artificial Intelligence

Artificial intelligence, AI, has, as a rule, a focus on creating intelligent computer systems, building models of how the brain works, and signal processing. It involves machine learning platforms, language processing, decision-making, speech, and vision recognition, promoting human–computer interaction (Kelly, 2015; Packard, 2018). AI emerged from searches for quick solutions to problems that are intellectually difficult to solve for humans (Goodfellow et al., 2016).

The current challenges are to teach systems to be intuitive according to a hierarchy of concepts (Goodfellow et al., 2016), but, still, there is a need for human intervention modeling mathematically the knowledge of the computer: AI processes a collection of characteristics from some object or event that we want the machine learning system to process (Goodfellow et al., 2016, p. 99). Therefore, the skills of a human being are provided to a machine learning algorithm: A performance measure is previously given for the system to execute a certain task (Goodfellow et al., 2016, p. 103).

1.2.1 Volition Versus Bias in the Use of AI

Artificial intelligence, AI, in its mathematical origin, presents itself as a rigorous, systematic, and deductive system, which is evolving to represent, in addition to the formal and abstract world, the sensitive and experimental world. While AI is perfected to imitate the human being in carrying out many tasks, previously modeled for this, it is seeking to endow it with the creative subjectivity of the human mind (Monte-Serrat et al., 2020), which is still a great challenge.

The human experience is always subject to doubt, making assumptions that cause effects the volition of the creative mind (Lloyd, 1907). Human intelligence, in its approaches to creating something new, involves cognition (intelligence, learning, memory, personality, and motivation) and the context of reality (Findlay & Lumsden, 1988). The much-sought creativity and innovation in scientific research depend on social influence (Warr & O'Neill, 2005); the recovery of information stored in memory (Gabora, 2002); and the relationship established between experience data and psychological or philosophical aspects (Bindeman, 1988). The researcher is therefore subject to a process in which they need to relate these elements, which is different from having 'ready-to-use' elements and information obtained from intelligent systems.

For there to be volition, the individual goes through a process of learning to interpret and produce ways of signifying, of conceiving the world (Padilha, 2000). This linguistic process to which human beings are subjected is what allows the latter to mean something other than what they were exposed to Lemos (2002). Thus, the individual researcher can develop characteristics of authorship, uniting coherently (and not a mere evaluation of rules) (Foucault, 1969) and with creative imagination, the content of their research, condensing meanings that are part of their experience, in a movement that merges categories that are part of sensitivity (Ostrower, 2013).

While scientific research harbors the creative thinking resulting from chance, from the event, it is also subject to strict methodological norms. The meaning and interpretation of the facts are regulated by social relations (Voloshinov, 1973). Research is associated with the social and cyber context and is, therefore, subject to regulation by both. On the one hand, science gives precedence to reason, making scientific thought 'sanitized' from 'unwanted' senses (Foucault, 1969; Levitt, 1996; Monte-Serrat, 2017; Pêcheux, 1975, 1988), through techniques aimed at incorporating certain points of view and rejecting others (Pêcheux, 1988). In this way, research can present a 'specialization' promoted by reason (Whorf, 1956) designed to incorporate certain points of view and reject others (Belgacem et al., 2019). This 'specialization' can be compared to the brushing technique in e-commerce (Monte-Serrat & Cattani, 2021b), which eliminates divergences so that the interpretation is aimed at a certain objective or meaning.

The brushing technique generalizes the interpretation, erasing certain particularities from the context (Monte-Serrat & Cattani, 2021; Wang et al., 2015). The researcher who makes use of the content offered on the Internet must be aware that the search systems for certain subjects brush the data, causing changes in the process of construction of the meaning of the subject in question, which may trigger an interpretive process unrelated to its context.

The volume of data stored by the system corroborates that the meaning of certain content tends toward a decontextualized (artificial) meaning, which favors the imposition of interest group perspectives (bias) (Monte-Serrat & Cattani, 2021).

In short, the sense/interpretation of reality, when influenced by intelligent search systems, can offer content and meanings detached from contextual reality (Foucault, 1969; Monte-Serrat, 2017; Monte-Serrat & Cattani, 2021; Pêcheux, 1975, 1988). This is because the search system is similar to the brushing technique, blurring some important details of the contextual reality that should be considered in the research; or because they are subject to the 'curse of dimensionality' (Goodfellow et al., 2016, p. 154), that is, being susceptible to bias due to the volume of information offered. These facts can, therefore, interfere in the interpretation, which becomes influenced by the closest data (Bengio et al., 2006; Monte-Serrat & Cattani, 2021; Wang et al., 2015) and not by the context that is the object of research.

1.2.2 Artificial Intelligence Tools and Plagiarism

Philosophizing the complex relationship between guiding and research nowadays, it is observed that there is a false belief that scientific research is increased by the facilities of the Internet, which offers a large volume of information and universal access (Magrani, 2019), establishing equal opportunities for researchers. Plagiarism, instead, has had its practice intensified through easy access to text search engines on the Internet, which act as enhancers of plagiarizing; even though they know that plagiarism has ethical and moral implications, researchers continue to plagiarize due to the practicality of finding ready-made texts, saving time and effort in developing content (Vasconcelos, 2007).

These negative effects of artificial intelligence tools on scientific research production led to increased rigidity in public and editorial policies, to the holding of world conferences on research integrity (Pithan, 2013; Vasconcelos, 2007). The importance of the topic of plagiarism in graduate school can be verified by the existence of publications from education regulatory bodies. In Brazil, the Coordination for the Improvement of Higher Education Personnel (Capes, 2011) recommends that Brazilian public and private educational institutions adopt policies of awareness and information on intellectual property, adopting specific procedures that aim to curb the practice of plagiarism. The same conduct was adopted by the São Paulo Research Foundation (FAPESP, 2014) and by the National Council for Scientific and Technological Development (CNPq, 2011).

The loosening of values caused by the misuse of the new tools of intelligent systems (CNPq, 2011) calls into question the concept of research, which was expected to be new and creative, making it 'petrified' (Arendt, 2011, p. 232). Harmful effects arising from fraud delay the advance of knowledge and cause damage to the economy and society (CNPq, 2011). Among these events, we can mention the rejection of principles of genetics, through the manipulation of data and information with ideological and political objectives, which brought delays in agricultural production; financial and human costs involved in correcting deviations; and damage to legitimate authors whose copyright was violated, among others (CNPq, 2011). In the context of scientific research, we bet on the mediation of the guiding professor, who, as a scale calibrator, can assume the role of balancing the values at stake in education.

1.3 Scientific Research: Efficiency and Productivity Versus Experience and Creativity

As the State is responsible for building agreements and rules that regulate education (Althusser, 2012), it must develop public policies that seek equity and quality of education in the country. The advisor in charge of conducting research, as a representative of the State, has the function of showing 'how' to build scientific knowledge in higher education. They must seek knowledge production with quality to escape the sameness of standards that only fulfill prerequisites to be achieved as goals.

On the one hand, there is the provision of digital library database resources, which have a significant impact on research in higher education, increasing research productivity and inspiring new academic policies to promote strategies that improve indexes (Rafi et al., 2019). On the other hand, young researchers expect that the intense use of ready-made information obtained through artificial intelligence for their discoveries will avoid repetitions of 'old' discoveries.

Although research activity at Academies and Institutes of Education is regulated and aimed at observing rigid objective schemes, this activity is also guided by the principle of research autonomy and by the individual originality to discover new frontiers (Belgacem et al., 2019).

On the State side, regulatory norms for research activity are observed, which presuppose responsibility and observance of principles. It is common to find public policies that establish, through a metric-bibliographic system, numbers, and indexes to be reached for the evaluation of research and researchers, such as the H index, Scopus, which, in turn, generates conflicts of interest related to the evaluation of renowned scientific journals in research (Belgacem et al., 2019). These criteria put pressure on academics and researchers to look for numbers, which, in our opinion, affects the creative content of research.

In addition to scientific decisions based on efficiency and productivity criteria, there are technological decisions based on concepts that may favor some groups or ideas over others. These biases may be embedded in neural devices (Yuste et al., 2017).

It is seen, therefore, that the definition of justice in research does not fit in mathematical rigor. Courtland (2018) states that although actuarial tools exist for valuations, large and complex numbers of data threaten ethical implications. One cannot throw information into the algorithms and ignore what happens to the results. The predictive parity, false positive, or false negative justice lose their raison d'être if there are differences between groups in the volume of data. Justice in one aspect is out of character if verified in another aspect.

On the advisor professor side, although they represent the State in the activity of guiding researchers, there is an interpersonal relationship that cannot be disregarded, making the orientation process grounded in regulations (State) and in trust, which encompasses the interpersonal relationship in which vulnerability or risk is accepted based on expectations regarding the behavior of another person (Williams, 2014; Belgacem et al., 2019; Costa & Frankhema, 2007).

Experience and creativity are developed under the tutoring process, which, although governed by rules and enriched by the tools of intelligent systems, extrapolates them, because it presupposes a personal exchange between advisor and researcher. This process occurs through the somatic and cognitive dimensions (Ricoeur, 1980; Merleau-Ponty, 1964) which interfere in the construction of the research content (Belgacem et al., 2019).

In summary, there is great complexity in the research activity. Doubt and the search for solutions are intrinsic to academic research. If the assumptions regarding the alternatives depend on the 'findings' of artificial intelligence, there may be decontextualization and bias in the content developed. If priority is given to the numbers of effectiveness and productivity, there is a risk that the content is not developed properly and does not show creativity. The latter, so highly valued in research, is based on interpersonal relationships, which, unfortunately, is losing ground to intelligent systems. Our best to avoid the scientific fragmentation caused by the volume of information from artificial intelligence at the expense of new and creative solutions is in the role of the advisor as a mediator.

1.4 Professor Advisor Acting as a Counterbalance

We investigate effective responses to the relationship between research and artificial intelligence assessing the values that are at stake in the search for appropriate solutions to the specificity of each case. In our opinion, the advisor, in their mission to tutor the researchers, assumes the role of a counterbalance, establishing proportion among some aspects: As a representative of the State, they must pay attention and comply with the pedagogical guidelines; as a good advisor, they must make good use of the tools of intelligent systems avoiding plagiarism and bias and, at the same time, encouraging creativity.

Principles and norms associated with the volume of content offered by the Internet do not guarantee creative and good-quality research. It is necessary to combine the 'culture of AI' with the 'culture of interpersonal exchange'. The guiding professor is fundamental to stabilizing all the elements to be considered (see Sects. 4.1, 4.2, and 4.3). In the activity of looking thoroughly to find excellence in research, they must think about the peculiarities of each case, reflect on the social transformations, ensure attention to the norms and rules of scientific research, and always provide the opening for creativity, seeking new solutions.

1.4.1 The Scientific Discourse

Monte-Serrat et al. (2017) shows that in the seventeenth century, logical reasoning presents itself as a mathematical structure in discourse. Decisions are made based on the choice of fragmentary information possibilities. Aristotle's formal logic is considered the basis of reasoning, interfering in decision-making to make them follow logical canons (Maldonato & Dell'orco, 2010). In this period of history, the systematic observation procedure was adopted, testing and modifying hypotheses and orienting the discourses toward an assumed condition (Pêcheux, 1988). This systematic reasoning, dependent on a set of techniques for making conjectures and predictions, values a 'determined' perspective to develop more sophisticated knowledge (Pêcheux, 1988; Peirce, 1877, 1908). This way of reasoning is developed through hypotheses based on pre-conceived knowledge and under controlled conditions (Pêcheux, 1988), determining and anticipating logical consequences. This is the functioning of scientific discourse which, with a hypothesis (if P) as an initial interpretation, gives an anticipated signification to other possibilities of meaning (then Q). There is a 'perceived truth' beforehand to eliminate alleged ambiguities (Monte-Serrat et al., 2017).

1.4.2 Qualitative Research: A Shift in the Value

Academic work involves the construction of knowledge to represent reality from a certain point of view. Thought categories considered as truths influence the positioning of researchers (scientific discourse). The balance between truth, regulation, and creativity in academic work will be found in qualitative research. The latter gives more importance to the transmission of information related to the context from which they were taken than to quantitative targets. This causes a shift in the value previously established by hypotheses ('if P', which guarantees processes crystallized by the reiteration of 'findings') to highlight issues that break this supposed transparency. Creativity, the novelty in scientific work, arises when the researcher realizes that, in addition to the sense previously established by the hypothesis, there are other possible meanings caused by specific production conditions in a specific context (Foucault, 1969; Pêcheux, 1975, 1988).

While in the scientific discourse, the tutor deals with the planning and implementation of methods and policies, checking the performance of researchers according to them, qualitative research offers opportunities beyond these previously established regulations. The quantitative method focuses on defining which policies to adopt and evaluate; qualitative methods, on the other hand, are concerned with the eventuality that the research objectives are met according to the context studied (Monte-Serrat et al., 2019).

In place of the quantitative data approach, of tests based on idealized parameters, the fourth-generation qualitative research (Campos & Furtado, 2011) proposes the observation of the problem along with the context in which it originated, escaping from standardized values. The qualitative approach of the research does not sanitize the data found but sustains the pluralities and can even become transformative actions in society (Campos & Furtado, 2011). This research practice refutes shelf studies due to their cooling, silencing, and paralyzing meaning for individuals and organizations (Patton, 1997; Silva & Brandão, 2011).

The relationship between contextual knowledge (experience), research (quantitative, qualitative methods), artificial intelligence, and researchers is mediated by the professor advisor.

1.4.3 Education as a Dynamic Process

Mediation is considered as the technical activity performed by a third party, chosen or accepted by the parties, to assist and encourage the development of a specific action in search of solutions to the controversy (concept adapted from Brazil, 2015).

The activity of the mediator implies the preservation of basic principles and rules (Takahashi, 2019). The task of distinguishing principles from rules is difficult: Principles are based on the fundamentality of some activity; the rules are based on the normative structure of the state (Takahashi, 2019).

In the case of the role of the professor advisor, as they are a representative of the State, they must act professionally to provide an adaptation of the research to the public interest and to the principles and norms in force in society. This tutor occupies the social position of someone who knows what are the conditions and the necessary care for research to be carried out successfully legitimately and appropriately.

The interpersonal relationship between the professor who directs the research and the researchers is the core of mediation. In this relationship, there is an informality (short form formalism) (Galanter, 1989) that guarantees the necessary procedural flexibility between the components involved, ensuring that a set of conditions are present and yet the freedom of action of the researcher and the advisor is guaranteed, without that it means giving up any rule. The mediator professor conducts communication with researchers, seeking to reconcile research activity with the use of artificial intelligence without ignoring current principles and norms and, at the same time, guaranteeing creativity in the findings.

In summary, the mediating activity of the advisor: (i) opens researchers to creative freedom in research, independence, and autonomy; (ii) is alert to avoid the practice of plagiarism; (iii) is attentive to the interference of bias due to the large volume of information provided by artificial intelligence; (iv) acts according to fundamental research principles, avoiding favoritism, preference or prejudice; and (v) ensures the application of the rules that regulate scientific research.

1.5 Conclusion

Research and artificial intelligence in the field of education imply values at stake. Great research opportunities arise all the time due to the speed and volume of information provided by intelligent systems. Research and creativity started to go hand in hand with plagiarism and bias due to changes brought about by the large volume of information circulating on the Internet.

The inattentive 'consumption' of this information by researchers can negatively influence human creativity, providing the researcher with a detached perception of reality, making the understanding converge to idealized preferences, and inducing decision rules that cause the elimination of 'uninteresting' solutions in favor of a previously given criterion.

Although research and artificial intelligence are the new reality of education, there are principles and values at stake that cannot be forgotten. We suggest that the role of the professor in charge of guiding research is the decisive core to avoiding the negative side of research activities and guaranteeing creative thinking as the basis for finding new paths.

There is still a lot to rethink about the incorporation of artificial intelligence in education. The advisor's responsibility as a mediator of this incorporation encourages opportunities for science and innovation to be socially sustainable, directing the benefits of research to the best for humanity.

References

Althusser, L. (2012). Ideology and ideological state apparatuses (notes towards an investigation). *Media and Cultural Studies: Keyworks, 80.*

Althusser, L. (2014). *On the reproduction of capitalism: Ideology and ideological state apparatuses.* Verso Trade.

Belgacem, F. B. M., Monte-Serrat, D. M., Cattani, C., & Cabella, D. M. S. (2019). Qualitative analysis of the academic work. *Educação&Realidade, 44*(4).

Bengio, Y., Delalleau, O., & Le Roux, N. (2006). The curse of highly variable functions for local kernel machines. *Advances in Neural Information Processing Systems, 18*, 107.

Bindeman, S. (1988). Echoes of silence: A phenomenological study of the creative process. *Creativity Research Journal, 11*(1), 69–77.

Brazil. (2015). Law No. 13,140, June 26, 2015. Provides for mediation between private individuals as a way of resolving disputes and the self-composition of conflicts within the scope of public administration. Retrieved from https://www.planalto.gov.br/ccivil_03/_ato2015-2018/2015/lei/l13140.htm. Accessed on April 25, 2021.

Campos, R., & Furtado, J. (2011). Desafios da avaliação de programas e serviçosemsaúde, Ed. Unicamp.

CAPES, Coordenação de Aperfeiçoamento de Pessoal de Nível Superior. (2011). (Coordination for the Improvement of Higher Education Personnel). Orientações de combateaoplágio (Guidelines for combating plagiarism). Retrieved from http://www2.ufac.br/ppgsc/documentos/orientacoes-capes-combate-ao-plagio. Accessed on April 20, 2021

CNPq, Conselho Nacional de DesenvolvimentoCientífico e Tecnológico. (2011). (Brazilian National Council for Scientific and Technological Development). Relatório da Comissão de

Integridade de Pesquisa (Research Integrity Committee Report). Retrieved from https://www.gov.br/cnpq/pt-br/composicao/comissao-de-integridade/relatorio-comissao--integridade-do-cnpq.pdf. Accessed on April 20, 2021

Costa, C., & Frankema, K. (2007). Trust and control interrelations: New perspectives on the trust—Control nexus. *Group & Organization Management, 32*(4), 392–406.

Courtland, R. (2018). The bias detectives as machine learning infiltrates society, scientists grapple with how to make algorithms fair. *Nature, 558*(7710), 357–360.

The Economist 2021. The world in 2021. Retrieved from https://www.economist.com/the-world-in-2021. Accessed on April 23, 2021

FAPESP, Fundação de Amparo à Pesquisa do Estado de São Paulo. (2014). (São Paulo Research Foundation). Código de boas práticascientíficas (Code of good scientific practice). Retrieved from https://fapesp.br/boaspraticas/. Accessed on April 20, 2021

Findlay, C., & Lumsden, C. (1988). The creative mind: Toward an evolutionary theory of discovery and innovation. *Journal of Social and Biological Structures, 11*(1), 3–55.

Foucault, M. (1969). *L'archéologie du savoir*. Gallimard.

Frankema, W., Raybeck, N., & Burbules, N. (2002). Philosophy of education. In J. Guthrie (Ed.), *Encyclopedia of education.*

Gabora, L. (2002). Cognitive mechanisms underlying the creative process. In *C&C 02 Proceedings of the 4th Conference on Creativity & Cognition*, pp. 126–133.

Galanter, M. (1989). Introduction: Compared to what? Assessing the quality of dispute resolution. *Denver University Law Review, 66*(3), 13–14.

Goodfellow, I., Bengio, Y., & Courville, A. (2016). *Deep learning*. MIT Press.

Haroche, C. (1984). *Faire dire, vouloir dire: La détermination et la désambiguïsation dans la grammaire* (Vol. 17). Presses Univ.

Henry, P. (1977). Le mauvaisoutil Langue, sujet et discours.

Kebritchi, M., Lipschuetz, A., & Santiague, L. (2017). Issues and challenges for teaching successful online courses in higher education: A literature review. *Journal of Educational Technology Systems, 46*(1), 4–29.

Kelly, J. E. (2015). Computing, cognition, and the future of knowing. *Whitepaper, IBM Research, 2.*

Lemos, C. (2002). Das vicissitudes da fala da criança e de suainvestigação (The vicissitudes of the child's speech and its investigation). In *Cadernos de EstudosLinguísticos, 42*, IEL-UNICAMP.

Levitt, N. (1996). Mathematics as stepchild of contemporary culture. In P. Gross, N. Levitt & M. Lewis (Eds.), *The flight from science and reason.* Annals of the New York Academy of Sciences.

Lloyd, A. (1907). *The will to doubt: An essay in philosophy for the general thinker*. S. Sonnenschein & Co.

Magrani, E. (2019). *Entre dados e robôs: ética e privacidadena era da hiperconectividade* (Vol. 5). Arquipélago Editorial.

Maldonato, M., & Dell'orco, S. (2010). Toward an evolutionary theory of rationality. *World Futures, 66*: 2, 103–123.

Merleau-Ponty, M. (1964). *The primacy of perception: And other essays on phenomenological psychology, the philosophy of art, history, and politics*. Northwestern University Press.

Monte-Serrat, D. (2017). Neurolinguistics, language, and time: Investigating the verbal art in its amplitude. *International Journal of Perceptions in Public Health, IJPPH, 1*(3).

Monte-Serrat, D., Belgacem, F., & Maldonato, M. (2017). Decision making: The complexity of choice processes. *International Journal of Research & Methodology in Social Science, 3*(4).

Monte-Serrat, D. M., & Cattani, C. (2020). Teaching in Online Classes: Social Presence from the Perspective of Michel Foucault and René Magritte. *People, 7*, 94.

Monte-Serrat, D. M., Cabella, B. C. T., & Cattani, C. (2020). The schrödinger's cat paradox in the mind creative process. *Information Sciences Letters, 9*, 1–10.

Monte-Serrat, D. M., & Cattani, C. (2021). Interpretability in neural networks towards universal consistency. *International Journal of Cognitive Computing in Engineering, 2*, 30–39.

Monte-Serrat, D. M., Khan, H. T., Kabir, R., Soares, D. W., & Silva, S. S. D. (2019). Reality and myth about legal healthcare support and quality of life in the Brazilian elderly. *Interface-Comunicação, Saúde, Educação, 23*, e190146.

Ostrower, F. (2013). *Acasos e criaçãoartística (Randomness and artistic creation)*, Ed. Unicamp.

Packard, H. (2018). Augmented intelligence: Helping humans make smarter decisions.

Padilha, A. (2000). Bianca. O ser simbólico (The symbolic being): Para além dos limites da deficiência mental. Ph.D. Thesis, Faculty of Education, UNICAMP, Brazil.

Patton, M. (1997). *Utilization-focused evaluation: the new century text* (3rd ed.). Sage Publications.

Pêcheux, M. (1975). *Les vérités de La Palice. Linguistique, sémantique, philosophie (Théorie)*. Maspero.

Pêcheux, M. (1988). *Discourse: Structure or event*. Illinois University Press.

Peirce, C. (1877). *The fixation of belief*.

Peirce, C. (1908). *A neglected argument for the reality of god*.

Pithan, L. H. (2013). Ética e integrida de napesquisa: o plágion as publicaçõe scientíficas. *Revista AMRIGS*.

Rafi, M., Jian Ming, Z., & Ahmad, K. (2019). Evaluating the impact of digital library database resources on the productivity of academic research. *Information discovery and delivery*.

Ricoeur, P. (1980) Narrative Time. *Critical Inquiry, 7*(1), 169–190. https://doi.org/10.1086/448093.

Silva, R., & Brandão, D. (2011), Nas rodas da avaliação educadora. In R. Campos & J. Furtado (Eds.), *Desafios da avaliação de programas e serviços em saúde*, Ed. Unicamp.

Takahashi, B. (2019). *Manual de mediação e conciliaçãonajustiça federal*. Conselho da Justiça Federal, Centro de Estudos Judiciários.

Vasconcelos, S. M. (2007). O plágionacomunidadecientífica: Questõesculturais e linguístcas. *Ciência e Cultura, 59*(3), 4–5.

Voloshinov, V. N. (1929). 1973. *Marxism and the philosophy of language* (L. Matejka & I. Tutunik, Trans.). Harvard University Press.

Wang, R., Purshouse, R., Giagkiozis, I., & Fleming, P. (2015). The iPICEA-g: A new hybrid evolutionary multi-criteria decision-making approach using the brushing technique. *European Journal of Operational Research, 243*(2), 442–453.

Warr, A., & O'Neill, E. (2005). Understanding design as a social creative process. In *C&C 05, Proceedings of the 5th Conference on Creativity and Cognition*. pp. 118–127.

Whorf, B. (1956). Language, thought, and reality. In J. Carroll (Ed.), *Selected writings of Benjamin Lee Whorf*, MIT Press.

Williams, T. (2014). The psychology of interpersonal trust. *How do people feel when it comes to trusting someone?. McKendree University, 22*, 1–17.

Yuste, R., Goering, S., Bi, G., Carmena, J. M., Carter, A., Fins, J. J., et al. (2017). Four ethical priorities for neurotechnologies and AI. *Nature News, 551*(7679), 159.

Chapter 2
Artificial Intelligence and Higher Education Legal Limits

Marius Vacarelu

Abstract Human knowledge has undergone a constant process of information accumulation—first about nature, then about space, and finally about most of the social processes in which a human being is involved during life. Obviously, not all this knowledge is exhaustive, but libraries are impressive witnesses to the work of so many generations of researchers and teachers, and no doubt we can appreciate it objectively as positive results in many areas. The evolution of knowledge has made a huge leap since the invention of printing, and from that moment, a growing category of people have access to knowledge about contemporary realities, as well as cultural and artistic "products". Knowledge has become increasingly "popular" in the background, meaning that the price of access to culture and information about every day realities has dropped to a level easily reached by more than half of each country's population. The second great transformation brought by the human mind appeared at the time of the Internet creation, which today has been extended to the dimension of new technology, called artificial intelligence. In this new paradigm, education is about creating new directions of action, and as a result, changing the entire human society. Within this great transformation, higher education—carried out in universities—will play a fundamental role, and the legal limits of the activities that these huge research centers are doing well in turn influence the next decades of all nations and countries, with no exception.

Keywords Artificial intelligence · Education · Legal framework · Transformation of society · Control and state purposes

2.1 Introduction

Higher education is appreciated by the whole society, but it has certain specificities that are sometimes more difficult to understand. This is the consequence of several factors, one of the most important of which is legislation.

M. Vacarelu (✉)
Faculty of Public Administration, National School of Political and Administrative Studies, Bucharest, Romania
e-mail: marius333vacarelu@gmail.com

F. Roumate (ed.), *Artificial Intelligence in Higher Education and Scientific Research*, Bridging Human and Machine: Future Education with Intelligence,
https://doi.org/10.1007/978-981-19-8641-3_2

For any young person, the idea of studying at a university became something natural and even necessary, especially in the period following the Second World War. The supreme price paid by almost 100 million people as well as the destruction of huge assets brought into question the widest possible reform of the political-administrative systems, and within them, the idea of transformation and widening access to universities appeared more than logical and necessary.

For centuries, higher education has not only a unique scientific prestige but also a specific attribute related to the intellectual and moral qualities of those who go through it, which makes the political environment have a certain reticence toward it. However, as the political environment is the one that creates the legislation in a country, this mistrust can be manifested by the appearance of different methods of restricting the freedom of expression and research of universities, as well as by other methods that affect the fulfillment of normal goals of these scientific entities—such as low funding, the creation of legal standards that are very difficult to achieve due to low funding, etc.

The emergence of information technology and then artificial intelligence has led to changes in the entire education system, and the pandemic that broke out in 2020 is forcing states and individuals to further implement new technological methods in education, to the detriment of the traditional style of knowledge provided to young people.

This technological-medical transformation forces more than ever the states and the political environment to be attentive to the higher education system regulation because this dimension of the society is responsible for the creation of the majority of the political-economic elites. Or, the way of working in these years of transition to the new technology of artificial intelligence—which will be fixed by legal norms—will have effects for the next decades, and no country can afford to fail in this process of cultural-educational transition.

It will be especially important to find a way to unify legitimate and traditional desires of a political and administrative environment with what only artificial intelligence can create. In the absence of this agreement between the two parties, a real conflict can be reached between the demands of the political environment and the artificial intelligence operators, and the greatest pressure will be borne by governments and parliaments because they cannot act with the same degree of coherence which new information technologies have.

2.2 The Research Methodology

The research methodology of this paper combines an analytical, historic-teleological, fundamental, conceptual, qualitative, and conclusion-oriented endeavor. Given the complexity of the topic, the research methods were used both individually and together, concerning the information context under analysis. Fundamental, qualitative, and historic-teleological researches were used to identify social, economic, or political trends that affected the whole educational system, trying to describe the complex equation of teaching and learning. Conceptual research is essentially associated with the description of educational processes so the relationship between them and artificial intelligence could be best described in terms of this methodology.

Being an analytical researcher, I started to search among facts or information available, analyzing them to realize a critical evaluation of the vast documentary, and underlining the main lines of the legal framework in education and artificial intelligence.

The vast dimension of the literature devoted to education, as well as the growing proportion of works dedicated to artificial intelligence force the researcher to focus his work on highly applied research, from which to draw the type of conclusions, or to seek to identify the force lines of the historical and contemporary realities in education. Thus, the researcher's efforts favored the conceptual and fundamental approach to the researched topic, looking for the overall picture of the national educational policies.

Therefore, the research is fundamental and oriented toward wide-ranging conclusions, which would allow the identification of trends in terms of both history and the future of education.

Our text seeks to answer a major question, namely that of the legislators' behavior in the face of modern technology challenges. In identifying the possible answers, the broad methodology of legal research was used, which must provide the direction for formulating the new principles and norms of law in higher education and their relationship with artificial intelligence.

The methodology of creating normative acts must capitalize on both the broad perspectives of legal sciences and those of ethics, because the action of legislation cannot reach the optimal level in the absence of the application of the ethical principles. Formal law presupposes a legal analysis quality finesse reached at the superior level because the results of disregarding its principles can bring major prejudices on the scale of an entire nation.

An important aspect to emphasize regarding the result of the legal methodology application is the temporal aspect, which is oriented toward the future, because until now, the national legislation had to regulate the digital realities of the twenty-first century only in a minimal form. Thus, the role of the researcher is to determine what will be the challenges that all legislators will face in the coming decades, identifying the fundamental issues that students, professors, universities, the labor market, and the social environment should understand and solve.

2.3 Basic Theory of Education

It is difficult to write about the issue of education, because—unlike other human activities, such as working in a nuclear power plant and researching the depths of the oceans—here, the author will constantly meet readers with their own opinions.

This is primarily because education is compulsory in all states, and each person has gone on a longer or shorter period of his life through the education system of their country—and in recent decades, even through educational institutions from other countries. On the other hand, working in a nuclear power plant is not accessible to everyone, although its effects are seen in energy prices for people and companies; researching the depths of the oceans involves very expensive equipment that is not accessible to any scientific entity, etc.

An important consequence of the way one writes about education is the rather controversial nature that certain opinions about education can have. Practically, any person can formulate his opinions, based on personal experiences—an aspect that cannot be neglected in this matter—and part, they can be considered that those opinions are grounded in a certain proportion (Paun, 2019, p. 14).

In addition, compared to the same systems presented above—working in nuclear power plants or researching the depths of the oceans—education has two fundamental issues, which make the number of variables in the analysis very large.

The first is that of human nature in itself. People are not the same, and this is evident in any field of activity. Or, changing psychological skills—mainly in the sense of growing or creating new ones—takes time and is done differently within each person. One person can learn very well through auditory stimulation, another through study in maximum silence; one young person can learn better based on patterns, and another based on a coherent narrative. Each person creates a part of the skills useful for education, and they will accompany him all his life. The same reasoning must be applied in terms of teachers' work style, even if they work at the same level, in the same institution, or even in the same year of study (Cucos, 1999, p. 11). The style is the man himself—as Buffon said—and in the education process, the teacher must somehow adapt to the pupils or students in front of him, being at the same time the man of his schemes of thinking and offering knowledge to others.

The second big difference is that general education begins at an early age, and education for matters of great finesse—nuclear research, deep ocean, etc.—often begins after reaching an age closer to maturity. As a result of this second form of education (physics, oceanography, etc.), those who go through it know from the beginning what they are doing—an aspect that no child aged seven can understand and predict.

This means that the destination of the child and adolescent in the educational and then professional sphere is not a perfectly controllable one, having multiple variations, based on different internal factors—medical, intellectual—or external, of which those of an economic nature are essential. These variations can also appear from the perspective of the quality of the educational activities provided by different teachers—some of which attract pupils and students to their subjects—and in other situations, we will find influences from the perspective of family traditions, which narrow the child's options from the first study years (Enachescu, 2011, p. 38).

There are great differences in the education system from two other perspectives, which are the expression of political will at a given time.

First, we will examine the basics of the education separation between that achieved through state schools and that made by the various forms of private education—either of a theoretical/scientific nature or a religious nature. It should be mentioned that these forms of education are specific—almost always—to a democratic political regime, in which legality is not a concept only mentioned on paper. Within this great differentiation, the particular systems are more mobile relative to the way of hiring the teachers, the different study programs, and the accessing of funds. From this perspective, these schools can function with very good results, if the financial aspect is consistent. After all, these financial differences—often expressed by the level of tuition fees—produce results and separations both from state schools and especially in the competition between these private schools. However, the financial aspect can also lead to the closure of this type of school or university, in the situation where the general results are not appreciated by graduates and society in general, so that at some point, the university rankings may experience changes due to this aspect. As an example, we could give the situation of a university whose main donor goes bankrupt, and which is thus forced to reduce its activity for a year or more, and what was lost in that period—teachers, programs, disciplines—cannot be recovered later (Matei, 2015, p. 29).

Within this system of private schools, there are two major subdivisions, both related to political will.

First, schools of a religious nature are not always appreciated by states, because in many situations, they are the schools of national minorities—less often belonging just to religious minorities. Or, in this situation, the religious schools also play an ethnic role—to strengthen the national element—and the study programs are not always completely confessional by nature but can also have strictly based on ethnic differences nuances. In this situation, we refer to a legal framework in which minorities are not persecuted, but only viewed with distrust by the majority ethnic group.

However, there are also situations in which the political regime does not trust a numerically consistent minority, and in this situation, it will not approve schools teaching in the language of that minority, nor forms of religious schooling dedicated strictly to an ethnic group considered to be secondary. In this situation—often encountered in history—minorities have created private schools and universities, illegal in terms of the legal framework established by the majority ethnic group in a country. In these illegal schools/universities, it was educated an important part of the youth, and as the result, the linguistic and religious aspects maintained. One of the best-known examples is that of Poland in the nineteenth and twentieth centuries (Davies, 2005, vol. II) because the division of the country and the way the Poles were seen by the three empires that had fully taken over the territory led to the natives to create a parallel education system, used by millions of children and teenagers. The system was the adversary of the political powers of the time and functioned exclusively based on the ethnic Poles' finances with great success, confirmed in 1918 year when Poland reappeared on the political map of the world. There have been many other cases of this type, and today's political and technological contexts favor education outside the legal and administrative state framework, so that parallel teaching–learning systems can have a more consistent existence in the following decades.

The analysis of schools created and financed entirely by the state is the most important, being in terms of numerical size the most in a country because schooling is mandatory in all countries of the world. In terms of funding, the issue of the school's operation is dual, because they will always have a minimum annual budget, which is often equalized, based on various legal rules. Budgeting on the number of pupils/students—each being from a budgetary point of view considered equal to all the others—ensures the annual functioning of all schools at the same minimum level of performance (Fartusnic, 2014, p. 53). We must also mention that in any country, there are schools and universities considered to be elitist, and for them, the budget allocations are higher. However, the existence of the state school system mainly induces equality within society, without excluding additional forms of training.

There are—unfortunately—even now a big number of less democratic countries; according to Freedom House criteria, 112 from 195 states are counted as authoritarian or not-fully democratic (Freedom House, 2020). History reveals that the predominant way of governing national communities was authoritarian or even dictatorial, in which the will of the ruler of the country—whether he was named king, emperor, or president—had the power of law over any other person, without any ways to correct/cancel the supreme leader's wishes. We must underline that states with a deficit of democracy reveal themselves as entities that usually act in a coordinated way in most social spheres, always pursuing—among other purposes—the loyalty of the population toward the leader (de Mesquita & Smith, 2011, p. 84). In this sense, several means will be used, and of these one of the most important is the national education system.

The totalitarians transform a large part of the educational process itself into a school for their particular ideology. The entire educational process is utilized for the propaganda efforts of the regime and is part of this purpose in ever-larger measure as the totalitarian nature of the dictatorship unfolds. Like the case, almost no criticism is possible under a totalitarian dictatorship. Teachers and pupils alike are continually exposed to the pressures emanating from the totalitarian party and its associated mass organizations. And when, in the course of the dictatorship's development, more and more teachers become absorbed into the movement, often by formal recruitment into the party itself, the distinction between education and propaganda becomes increasingly blurred, as far as broadly moral and social fields of study are concerned. Education, like ideology, becomes an instrument in the hands of the regime that takes upon itself the definition of the truth. This process reached its extreme point in Stalin's—and Mao, later (a.n.)—celebrated concern with language (Friedrich & Brzezinski, 1965, p. 146).

Totalitarian regimes purge the professor's corpus, try to recruit the most popular of them, and send to jail the ones who are revealing truths about the state regime and daily situations. Pupils are encouraged to report about any possible form of opposition or critics inside the school, society, and even family: as an example, in the former European communist world, the Pavlik Morozov case—when a young boy reports to authorities about some "illegal" actions of his family and as result, his father was executed—was appreciated by the Soviet state and is story was spread in all communized country after 1945.

Education, culture, and art have always been closely related, and as an effect, the educational process was directed toward state-approved art. One element of totalitarian culture and art which is shown to open up for genealogies reaching far beyond the strictly totalitarian sphere is the heroization of work, a feature just as prominent in fascist and communist regimes. The heroization of work again hovers ambiguously between the futurist embrace of technology and archaizing ruralism, fetishizing instrumental artifacts simultaneously with raw muscle power and by this means re-evoking the militant youth culture of classical antiquity (Rassmusen & Wamberg, 2010, p. 10).

2.4 Education Between Quality and Quantity

Education is an ongoing process, made clear not only by specialists in the learning sciences—but especially in our lives, where a good part of the errors and failures we encounter is the consequence of knowledge we did not meet in advance.

The educational process is limited in time—several weeks in a year and several life years. What the Latins taught us—Nonscholae, sed vitae discimus/we are learning for life, not for school—is at the same time an exhortation, but also a warning about the need to exercise this process for a practical purpose, outside of school.

These two major aspects are complemented—at least in the last two decades—by the result of the huge technological advance that mankind has made. This means that the technological change of the last decades has appeared rather abruptly—relative to the other great advances in science—but with results that have disrupted to a large extent the old ideas about education (Ceobanu, 2016, p. 17).

First, we will examine the issue of the educational calendar and the ages of those who reach the classical schooling system. The number of study days is not the same in all countries, although it generally covers more than half of the 52 weeks of the year. Climate conditions influence the school calendar, and how the learning process which is done is different in this regard, because—objectively—not all schools in the world are provided with high-performance air conditioning, and this lack of tools is just one of the education system underfunding symptoms. Financial strains mean that in some countries, the duration of schooling is shorter because the state simply cannot afford a longer duration of courses; this budget shortage is often accompanied by fairly high dropout rates (Landes, 1999, p. 31).

The biggest problem that policymakers have with the educational system is the length of their studies in years, and especially the lower and upper limits that they can reach. Here, several wishes and opinions are confronting, because partly, the society and the economic environment want to have young people aged 23–24 very skilled, but the parents who have to bear most of the top education costs want an efficient school program, less loaded with information, but better taught by teachers. The optimum is to have very well-trained and popular teachers so that students can learn in all years of primary and secondary school—when most of the intellectual skills of the future adult are formed—with pleasure increasing the amount of information. However, this optimum is impossible to achieve, because the "distribution" of valuable teachers is numerically and spatially limited so that some schools will always be ahead of others. Because of these spatial and numeric characteristics, the graduates do not have a unitary level in the national area, even the society and the economic environment expect well-skilled young people, to be very able to enter the labor market.

Realizing that there are more and more requirements on the labor market, legislators have begun to lower the age at which the actual process of learning to read and write, basic mathematics, a foreign language, etc., begins. However, lawmakers need to keep in mind that between the ages of three and five, the child's mind may not contain as much information as some abstract planners in ministerial offices would like, and the fatigue will begin to set in at an early age. The tender will lead to exhaustion over time because the human brain should not be treated as a machine with constant operation for decades (Panisoara, 2011, p. 41).

There is also the problem of upper limits of study years because the same economic environment requires graduates who have solid knowledge in as many domains as possible. However, today, the available amount of scientific and practical/professional information is huge, and its complete traversal is impossible. The need to know as much as possible is real, and in many domains, today's work is very sophisticated, requiring all those involved in it a high level of knowledge, which can be obtained only after many years of intense study. Or, this need to know before entering the labor market brings into question the number of study years in universities, as well as the optimal time when a graduate can be considered truly prepared for the needs of today's economy. Although this question is much more flexible and more difficult for the legislator to regulate, it is still true that a graduate in the 1930s should have known less than a contemporary student—and this is very clear in the field of technical sciences.

One of the latest reports from UNICEF and the European Union (UNICEF, 2020) reveals the growing dissatisfaction of children and adolescents on the continent relative to their socio-economic expectations, and one of the reasons for this result lies in not adapting educational systems to major technological and medical changes met in recent years.

In this perspective, it is necessary to briefly examine the issue of the physical dimension of the Internet and the human brain. Never before has such a large amount of useful information been so readily available to both school and economics professionals. For this reason, it can be considered that the universal library called the Internet has reached a degree of expansion that no physical construction could accommodate. However, if the quantity of information has increased—implicitly, the possibility of reaching it—the same cannot be said about the human brain, much less about the brains of children and adolescents. The adaptation of contemporary man to the Internet is not possible now, relative to the capabilities of our brains, and to demand that children and adolescents can understand, distinguish, and select the most appropriate information from this huge universal library is inappropriate to reality.

The quantitative dimension has become very well represented, because the amount of information that the Internet offers are increasing daily, at a level unimaginable a century ago. The distinction between the universal library called the Internet and general libraries—whether those of schools and universities or those of large cities—needs to be made, of the very small space that digital technologies occupy in a house, which would have been very burdensome for a normal home if those e-books had been in print. Housing prices in urban areas are high and every thousand books downloaded for free from the Internet would have claimed a suitable space in a house, or even a room dedicated strictly to storing books—in case, the owner had more than 5000 volumes. Or, the Internet offers this spectacular attraction: to be able to have 100,000 books in a storage space smaller than a table where you eat breakfast in bed.

There is a huge problem: The human brain is not static, and it is not functional in the same way at every moment of the day, and—especially—it can have different forms of blockage. The Internet offers access to information, but without reading it, the brain remains at the same stage of knowledge, and we must underline that in the educational process, the idea of reading mandatory and optional bibliographies is eternal (Burnett, 2016, p. 194). As long as it will not be possible to implant an electronic form in the human brain at the same time for all inhabitants of our planet, the only increase will be access to information, but not effective knowledge.

Even though access to books and scientific information is easier today, it does not mean that reading could be replaced, and the joy of reading texts is not created when the human being has reached the age of 25 or more. Increasing access to knowledge has become something that both teachers and students are aware of, but it does not mean that administrative curricula can change so much as to cover today's huge disproportion between what may be required by university exams and elite companies.

A company must adapt to today's economic realities and may not want to hire people who have adapted training in the 1990s or 2000s, and in this sense, they will ask potential employees to know at 23–25 years what one century ago professionals with 20 or 30 years of experience knew. Thus, for hundreds of years, we have been facing an upward trend in the amount of scientific information required of pupils and students, concerning the logical demands of employers, but this increase is not in line with the functioning capabilities of the human brain.

From this perspective, we can better understand the dimension of the higher education concept. Specifically, 100 years ago, a student at a technical university—for example, in civil engineering—had to know things that were technologically available to his country, keeping in mind that the differences from the industrial capacities of other countries in the world were not extraordinary. Today, a student must know advanced technologies, not necessarily available in their country—but which may be useful to him, because the labor market is globalized in many areas. The Internet is fundamental to achieving this goal—namely to know the most advanced technologies in a field—but quantitatively, it is clear that this scientific progress has in the mandatory bibliography many more books than the student of the 1920s had. At the same time, the day also has 24 h, and brain fatigue is not a process that begins on the first day of university, but much earlier if a young person wants to study at an elite college/university.

In short, we can say that the Internet century is that of the confrontation between quantity and fatigue because it is not enough to have access to something; we must be able to understand what we have access and then to use those issues in such a way that man not to be crushed by fatigue or other phenomena that could create a mental disorder or even the body dysfunctions (Varghese & Mandal, 2021, p. 8).

The issue of quantity is accompanied by that of quality. If for thousands of years, there were not enough materials to know the different scientific information desired; now, we are faced with a unique situation, in which for most areas of activity, we find abundant information. It should be noted, however, that not all countries will be able to find the same freedom of access to information because dictatorial systems block some data that is not comfortable with the regimes in power. Even in those countries, information is abundant in many fields, usually in technology, industry, and agriculture.

It is necessary to understand the definition of quality in education, as well as to understand the relationship between quality and the amount of information. Because we are not in the technical sphere, where the parameters are easy to measure and buy, we will find an expression of quality in education being more fluid, without fixing it in a fully measurable framework—although scientometrics and other forms of scientific work evaluation can be considered as a form of quality measurement.

It must be borne in mind that policymakers and state legislation must follow the idea of quality in education and less so that of quantity. It is true that in many various organizations' official documents, the quality of education will be considered to be increasing based on quantitative indicators, but—in our opinion—this is not the correct definition of the concept.

Firstly, we must mention a dictionary definition: Quality as contained in Oxford Advanced Learner's Dictionary—published in 2010—means the standard of something when it is compared to other things like it; how good or bad something is.

UNESCO highlights the importance of the quality of education offered in schools, showing that quality in education will later provide the beneficiary with higher incomes and increased professional satisfaction. The higher quality of educational institutions improves students' cognitive skills that directly influence future earnings, labor productivity, and overall economic growth. Currently, educational institutions also play an essential role in developing non-cognitive characteristics among students, such as honesty, responsibility, determination, and empathy. Educational institutions play an instrumental role, being a means by which individuals achieve their own socio-economic and cultural objectives contributing to the development of society (UNESCO, 2005).

Education is a way of providing every student with the intellectual means and cultural capital to keep learning after school/university.

We propose a definition of quality in education, related to the contemporary situation of technology and the labor market, as well as to the old Latin dictum of learning for life, and not for school/university grades. Thus, we will consider quality in education as the fulfillment of a large process of knowledge and skills accumulation, useful to life and professions at a level that would make the graduate accepted at the top 10 companies within a country.

Quality is, therefore, a process of knowledge accumulation to their proficient use, which each year becomes wider—because the knowledge needed to reach the level desired by the strongest employers is constantly growing. Thus, the process of increasing the quality of education is largely controlled by employers and less by schools and universities. This can be concluded from the fact that adults go-to forms of professional training long after completing the classic school-university study cycle because modern professions today require huge amounts of information, which are not always able to perform in school units—time-limited in their activities by the compulsory legal framework.

However, the quality of education is obtained by summing up several elements, some of which are strictly related to the legal framework, others to the activity of the authorities in the field, and others are related to the effort of the student and his/her family.

The legal framework is the one that must ensure a level as close as possible to equality in terms of a child's developmental changes, and in this sense, we have in mind both the spaces and textbooks that schools use, but also the provision of scholarships for children from less financially developed families. Again, we will emphasize that perfect equality between people cannot exist, and in this regard, we must keep in mind that the performance of a child from a poor family will often be weaker than that of a child from a family with a substantial income, because the diet is different, and it has effects on brain capacity; the capacity to travel and to visit museums and cultural buildings is different; books from own house are in a different number, etc. We must underline that at the country level, the legal framework must take into account both the assurance of the greatest chances of development of each child—and not only of equality of chances between them. This does not exclude the creation of elite schools, in whose spaces only students who pass difficult exams will study. Stimulating competition between students—a fundamental aspect of success in education—is necessary for the same theme of education for life, where we know very well that not everyone manages to become a billionaire or CEO of an oil company.

Institutions in the field of education—those in the vertical ministerial structure, complemented by private entities operating in this area—must bear in mind that quality assurance cannot be done without careful supervision of the entire system. But this cannot solve the whole quality of education problem; thus, it is more than necessary to include this learning scheme in a close—and sometimes difficult—partnership with the students' families, because they have to take care of the children's way in those hours when the young person left the school space. It is one of the biggest mistakes relative to the quality of education to not take into account the child's effort when he is not in the school building. Although it is fashionable to talk about "children's freedom" or even "eliminating the oppression of children", the economic reality is unmistakable: Employers want well-trained people, related to the scientific information amount available, which makes this goal of "good training" to require much more knowledge than was necessary few decades ago—before the Internet creation. Yes, there is a need to prevent brain fatigue in people who have not yet reached maturity, but their future cannot be sacrificed for an extra hour of play in nature. If life were according to our desires—perfectly selfish, but legitimate—no one would work but would benefit free from everything he wants. This equation is the description of a utopia and any attempt to create a system close to this desideratum would have effects: laziness, economic inefficiency, poverty, and the loss of potential brilliant minds. Therefore, this reduction of free time must be done intelligently, with the lowest possible costs, because learning costs not only time but also money: The intellectual elite needs books in the school bibliography addition, and not all of them are subsidized by state budgets. For this reason, in the next years, the children number per family may decrease in almost all countries—the costs of education are high and can be extremely burdensome for not always consistent budgets of many families.

The qualitative dimension of education is becoming more and more quantitative because reaching a level of proficiency in any area means—cumulatively—knowing information and using it most properly. If the mental and professional scheme of information use can be learned in school, the increasing amounts of data make this matrix constantly growing, which requires memorization augmentation, with the direct effect of time reduction for rest and recreation. Learning does not only mean knowing where to look for information because the question arises: What can a person with good information skills do if the Internet is disconnected for several hours? Reformulating the question: Can the Internet and free access to it supplement the idea of memorizing scientific information? Direct and concrete answer: no.

2.5 Artificial Intelligence in Higher Education. Legal and Moral Limits

The very rapid development of information technology has the effect of spreading knowledge from most spheres of human activity to a level unknown by history. This increase has been accompanied by the provision of very wide access to information to a very large percentage of the planet's population—5.053 billion Internet users at the end of 2020, representing 65% of the world population (Internet World Stats, 2021)—at a very low price. Based on this spread of information technology, the work of research institutes has finally led to the creation of a new form of technology, namely that of artificial intelligence.

Artificial intelligence did not suddenly appear and was being anticipated by many writers and scientists. However, in the perspectives, they imagined—and the writers were the most descriptive in this regard—artificial intelligence is often described as "the perfect tool", "the supreme means by which human physical and mental limitations will be overcome"—a real panacea, which will turn the life of the whole planet for the better. Obviously, in these perspectives, the sphere of education will also benefit from the technological progress brought by artificial intelligence, so that for the first time in history, education will be something pleasant for students and teachers.

These perspectives are beautiful to put on paper, but they have no real connection with the world we live realities. The technological, economic, and legal conditions are different in each country, which indicates from the beginning differences in the adoption of any new idea/product, and this international gap has important effects on education too.

A legal definition of artificial intelligence is found in US legislation: "(A) Any artificial system performs tasks under varying and unpredictable circumstances without significant human oversight or can learn from experience and improve performance when exposed to data sets. (B) An artificial system developed in computer software, physical hardware, or another context that solves tasks requiring human-like perception, cognition, planning, learning, communication, or physical action. (C) An artificial system designed to think or act like a human, including cognitive architectures and neural networks. (D) A set of techniques, including machine learning, is designed to approximate a cognitive task. (E) An artificial system designed to act rationally, including an intelligent software agent or embodied robot that achieves goals using perception, planning, reasoning, learning, communicating, decision-making, and acting" (US Congress, National Security Commission on Artificial Intelligence, 2018).

AI may be characterized as artificial narrow intelligence (ANI), artificial general intelligence (AGI), and artificial superintelligence (ASI). ANI is depicted as "weak" intelligence because it concerns the performance of a singular task that it generally accomplishes very well, e.g., playing chess against human experts, making sales predictions, autonomously driving automobiles, and may, at this juncture, include speech and image recognition. "Weak" is used in the sense of its limitation to one task rather than having a broader usage. AGI, also known as "strong AI" or "human-level AI", is the next higher level of AI progression in that it seeks to imitate the human brain, albeit its development continues to lack the reasoning and other attributes of the brain. ASI is a futuristic characterization that will disputably occur when AI has surpassed the capacity of the human brain in creativity, social skills, and wisdom. This last development poses unique challenges that potentially are extraordinarily beneficial or detrimental to society. Whether a particular robot is either an ANI or AGI depends on whether it meets the Turing test standard (Turing test is a method of inquiry in artificial intelligence for determining whether or not a computer is capable of thinking like a human being), i.e., whether its behavior resembles that of human and other measures. The more it resembles a human person, e.g., one working on an assembly plant, the more likely it would be characterized as an AGI (Girasa, 2020, p. 10).

While most interests are related to ASI, this level of artificial intelligence is more difficult to achieve in this decade—but research progress may reach this level as well. We must mention that ASI is also "attractive" from the perspective of the fact that today science is no longer something "esoteric", the prerogative of the tribe's healers. Thus, the science spread on a very wide level is also doubled by literature and in the mind of every man thoughts inspired by his scientific knowledge are mixed with thoughts inspired by the books read. Or, the mind not being temporally structured—"from 9 to 12 I think scientifically, from 12 to 15 I think inspired by fiction, from 15 to 18 I think inspired by political events"—it is logical for a man to consider all the dimensions of his intellectual personality in every problem analyzed. As the most widespread literature—scientific or fiction—about ASI, it will dominate the minds of most people, as well as part of the political discourse, being decisive in the legislation governing artificial intelligence adoption.

Today, we are in the presence of the first two forms of artificial intelligence—ANI and AGI, which cause today enough worries to the legislators for thinking of a supplementary regulation of ASI. In the field of education, this differentiation is very important, because only a few institutions with special financial strength can afford to research on a scale that could facilitate the emergence of ASI. The importance of ASI is seen today, especially from a political and military perspective, while ANI and AGI are considered from a broader perspective, relative to the fact that in some areas, these two forms are applied by different operators.

The regulation of artificial intelligence in education is influenced by three factors: the economic power of the country that adopts the new legal framework; the cycle—the school or university—legislator has in mind; the type of artificial intelligence to which a country/educational institution may have access.

Artificial intelligence is a new technology, not available in the same way in every country. The devices needed for this are still expensive for a part of the planet's population. A well-known phenomenon from economic history is applied again: Someone creates one new technology and exploits it alone for a while, gaining a quasi-monopoly on the market; after years or decades, other economic actors appear in this area, being forced to work hard to achieve a good market quota.

In education, the introduction of new technological tools is gradual in every country, and a country with a GDP/capita of $5000 will implement the technologies that a country with a GDP of $30,000 per capita used 5–10 or even 15 years ago. Thus, the regulations of artificial intelligence follow today an economic framework that can be achieved mainly by a third of the world countries. This limitation is because out of an average global GDP of $10,914, only 65 states out of 195 have reached it (IMF, 2020); it should be noted that close to this value, there are several other states—some with dictatorial or authoritarian political regimes—that will make efforts to promote artificial intelligence. Thus, most countries will not have access to the entire political and economic framework resizing because they lack the money needed to implement this technology.

The relationship between higher education and artificial intelligence is not simple, because this technology can greatly affect the ethics of education, both objectively—based on economic differences between students, and subjectively—based on students' attitudes toward task fulfillment. Thus, the regulation of this relationship must be done very carefully, considering first of all the ethical aspect, because the economic one is impossible to control—the differences in the wealth of families will be objectified by children's access to different books, tools, and technologies. As mentioned above, artificial intelligence is at the beginning of its "career", which makes some of its applications expensive for many persons who want them. Higher education legislation will therefore have to take into account that this economic aspect should be weighted by the ethical factor and not vice-versa.

Concerning these aspects, we will formulate the fundamental concerns that legislators must take into account in the matter of the relationship between artificial intelligence and higher education:

1. Artificial intelligence must be used in such a way as to help the development of human intelligence, increasing its thinking abilities. Artificial intelligence must not be used for the human mind capabilities replacing, nor to facilitate its work to the level where the most complex operations are performed exclusively through artificial intelligence;
2. The legislation must take into account as a supreme element the ethical aspect, subordinating its technical aspect. Thus, both teachers and students must keep in mind that the whole concept of artificial intelligence must be subject to ethical norms, and not just a part of it;
3. Legislation must take into account that artificial intelligence technology has not reached its limits, which means that some aspects of the legal framework will have to be regulated to allow the new technological developments integration. The reason for this flexible area of legislation lies in the fact that technologies are always developing faster than a parliament law, and in this context, we can reach the situation when universities cannot upgrade their own intelligent devices because the legislation does not allow this. As consequence, it will appear a gap to other research institutions and a decrease in the technological strength of the whole country;
4. Universities must keep in mind that artificial intelligence technology is still expensive and difficult to universally provide to the high school and secondary levels. Thus, a legal framework must be created to establish the rules from a traditional education system transition to one in which artificial intelligence plays a major or even fundamental role. This set of regulations is necessary because the transition between the two systems must be made gradually so that the implementation of education supported by artificial intelligence is not done by not solving the unavoidable knowledge deficits which appear during the traditional framework of the education route;
5. The legislation will have to adequately regulate the different typologies of teaching and learning for the socio-human sciences, on the one hand, relative to the technical sciences, on the other hand. This separation will have to be taken into account starting with high school education, bearing in mind that the universities will concretize the typology of teaching and learning differences between the two major branches of science;
6. Artificial intelligence will bring into question the resizing of learning in university buildings so that the implementation of this technology will lead to a reduction of the university spaces because some students will be able to learn from home. Thus, only the examinations may be done in university buildings, which will mean an increase in the number of buildings available to be used for different than education purposes. These possible spatial changes could bring into question

a change of the current regulations in the matter because there will be important patrimonial and financial consequences for the educational institutions;

7. Artificial intelligence will create in the coming decades an extraordinary separation of the national economies' development levels. Based on the new classifications of economies, it will appear new separations of education quality at the global level and will call into question the governmental recognition of the curricula and study documents;
8. As artificial intelligence use will increase in the coming years at all economic, administrative, and educational levels, it becomes necessary to adopt a set of legal measures for the situation in which there will be moments of energy crisis or disruption of digital systems for longer periods. The current coronavirus crisis has not been accompanied by energy or digital infrastructure crisis, but future clashes between states that will manifest themselves by blocking computer technologies—implicitly the use of artificial intelligence—are not excluded.

Therefore, the legislators must consider the creation of a legal framework to provide practical regulations for the public systems functioning—implicitly education—in the situation when energy and/or digital infrastructure is made impossible by operation for longer.

A specific question of the twenty-first century that legislation must answer is represented by the mission of universities. The role that these educational institutions must play in the artificial intelligence century—and electronic infrastructures, more correctly—can no longer be the traditional one, in which the essence of the activities is limited to teaching, learning, and trying to increase the intellectual and moral qualities of students (Engwall, 2020, p. 198).

The fundamental change that higher education will experience in this century is a direct consequence of artificial intelligence. Specifically, this technology will first increase the documentation capabilities of teachers and students, which will make the way of conducting educational activities, as well as the requirements for exams increase to an unprecedented level. Thus, it will appear a real new paradigm of academic excellence, in which both teachers and students will be required to be as close as possible to a perfect model of education.

The paradigm of perfection in education means that universities will have to have perfect teachers, who carry out the highest standards of both teaching and research—both categories will appear as a direct consequence of artificial intelligence's use. The students who will benefit from the activity of these teachers will have a graduation diploma that will certify the perfection of their work, which will make them unique in the labor market. All these aspects of perfection will be the consequence of artificial intelligence, which will bring with it possibilities that before no form of training could provide fully and undifferentiated. Thus, AI technology will be the one that will increase the capacities of all higher education actors system, which will bring major benefits to the new generations of employees, who will thus be privileged in front of the older generations operating in the labor market.

We will be facing a major separation of society, which will manifest itself in two areas. First, major changes will occur in the field of education, because artificial intelligence will be implemented rather at the university level, which will settle high school graduates on lower positions in future professional configurations. Secondly, the labor market will be separated in the coming decades between those who have completed their professional training with the help of artificial intelligence and others, who will act on other reflexes, with more mental skills, but also with more possibilities to make mistakes at work (Coleman, 2019, p. 62).

In both cases, the legislators must keep in mind that the chance of generations educated with the support of artificial intelligence does not turn into legal privileges. In addition, the legislation will have to provide for as many people as possible—and in some areas even the obligation—to take professional development courses, in which to learn in a short time the knowledge necessary to use artificial intelligence technology.

Working legislation will be strongly affected by the new digital technology, and companies' codes of ethics will have to provide clear boundaries regarding the distribution of employees and labor relations within. In addition, the fact that in all countries, there is an obligation to continue professional development, it will be necessary to adopt a legal framework to substantiate a relationship between companies and universities, because the enrollment figures in artificial intelligence technology will be high, and a strong pressure will be felt both by the labor market and the universities.

Two more issues need to be noted, both of them being consequences of the universities mission's problem in the twenty-first century.

First, a special effect of artificial intelligence will be found in politics, because perfectly educated people will be considered the best able to lead local communities and nations. Again, it will be the legislators' role not to create legal obstacles in front of those who want to climb the stair of public dignity, regardless of their degree of education. When artificial intelligence will become easy to use in a wide range of everyday life, universities will be called to ensure the perfection of future leaders, which will turn them into arbiters of the nation's future. Because not all universities will implement artificial intelligence technology at the same time, those that will have advanced in this direction will offer their graduates a major advantage in all spheres of public action, and this aspect will be known by the whole society (Ashri, 2020, p. 134).

Also, the mission of universities will be to imagine solutions for a world in which artificial intelligence could not function for a longer time at its normal parameters. Educational institutions must bear in mind that Einstein appeared after Pythagoras, and in the absence of the past century's science, we would not have reached the technological level of today. Thus, no matter how great and profound the transformation of our world will be in the coming decades, universities will have the mission to preserve the entire human science, precisely to teach their students those necessary solutions for the moments when this century's technologies will no longer work.

That is why we will consider that the mission of higher education in this century is the most complex possible—unprecedented in history—because it must create solutions to solve problems brought from the past and ideas for the development of humanity. However, these two goals must be achieved based on clear legal norms, which strengthen the role of ethics in people's lives, without turning the younger generations into cynical manipulators of digital technologies.

2.6 Conclusions

Artificial intelligence is now seen almost as a panacea: It is the medicine that makes any brain perform and see the solutions to any problem, even if so far no one has been able to identify it. Even if it does not have this role, it will profoundly change the lives of all people, forcing education systems—and especially higher education—to adapt to new lines of organization and action.

Most of the great inventions had as their initial purpose their applicability in the politico-military sphere, being only later used in the civil area. In all situations, the great inventions presupposed a higher education for their creators, an aspect impossible to evade in this century. Thus, new technologies are the essence of the university environment's abilities to intellectually train people who will develop their entire brain force in directions useful to society.

The challenges that artificial intelligence technology will bring are unique in the scale of history, which puts universities in dilemmas. Any university is aware that from its graduates can emerge either genius of science or people whose activities can harm a nation in the long run. For this reason, leaving only to the universities the ways of adapting and using the technology of artificial intelligence is naive and dangerous, because the age of 20 does not automatically bring wisdom and maturity to its users.

It is, therefore, necessary that the education legislation be adapted to the entire issue of artificial intelligence. Because it has extraordinary potential, it obliges all social actors to get involved, to establish a coherent set of legal norms and ethical principles, so that this technology implementation is not done in such a way as to consolidate the deficiencies in society.

Higher education is the last in a cycle that a person starts around age five. Before the invention of artificial intelligence, this age threshold functioned worldwide almost the same, because the teaching–learning methods were quite similar. Or, the emergence of this new technology can change the teaching methods applied to children from an early age, which will have the effect of a consistent differentiation: on the one hand, it will be those who have benefited in their education by artificial intelligence, and on the other hand, children who will use only classical methods, because their schools could not afford the AI costs. Implementation of this new technology will have to take into account that not all educational institutions will benefit from it at the same time. Thus, different levels will appear in the intellectual and professional development of the new generations, and legislators must find ways to harmonize the educational and professional typologies that will appear in the coming decades.

Legislation must be strengthened by ethical norms because it will be impossible to achieve social cohesion in a situation where for various reasons, some groups will have too many advantages over the average. A correct proportion between ethics and legality will prove useful to all citizens, and the benefits will be reflected in the whole society—of course, further research is needed to formulate the most effective relationship between these two important institutions of social life.

References

Ashri, R. (2020). *The AI-Powered Workplace: How Artificial Intelligence, Data, and Messaging Platforms Are Defining the Future of Work*. Apress Springer Group.

Burnett, D. (2016). *The idiot brain*. Faber and Faber.

Ceobanu, C. (2016). *Invatarea in mediul virtual: Ghid de utilizare a calculatorului in educatie*. Polirom.

Coleman, F. (2019). *A human algorithm: How artificial intelligence is redefining who we are*. Counterpoint Press Perseus Group.

Cucos, C. (1999), *Pedagogie*. Polirom.

Davies, N. (2005). *God's playground. A history of Poland, Vol. II*. Columbia University Press.

de Mesquita, B. B., & Smith, A. (2011). *The dictator's handbook: Why bad behavior is almost always good politics*. Public Affairs Perseus Group.

Enachescu, E. (2011). *Invatarea continua: Aplicatii la educatie si invatamant*. Editura Universitara.

Engwall, L. (2020). *Missions of Universities. Past, present, future*. Springer.

Fartusnic, C. (ed.). (2014). *Finantarea sistemului de invatamant preuniversitar pe baza standardelor de cost. O evaluarea curenta din perspectiva standardelor de cost*. UNICEF & Institute for Education Sciences, Vanemonde.

Freedom House. (2020). *Freedom in the World 2020. A leaderless struggle for democracy*. Retrieved from https://freedomhouse.org/report/freedom-world/2020/leaderless-struggle-democracy

Friedrich, C. J., & Brzezinski, Z. K. (1965). *Totalitarian dictatorship and autocracy*. Harvard University Press.

Girasa, R. (2020). *Artificial intelligence as a disruptive technology. economic transformation and government regulation*. Palgrave Macmillan.

International Monetary Fund. (2020). *World economic outlook (October—2020). List of countries by projected GDP per capita*. Retrieved from http://statisticstimes.com/economy/countries-by-projected-gdp-capita.php

Internet World Stats. (2021). *Internet world stats. Usage and population statistics*. Retrieved from https://www.internetworldstats.com/stats.htm

Landes, D. S. (1999). *The wealth and poverty of nations: Why some are so rich and some so poor*. W.W. Norton & Company.

Matei, C. S. (2015). *Morala, educatie, comunicare in era focului rece*. Tritonic.

Panisoara, G. (2011). *Psihologia copilului modern*. Polirom.

Paun, E. (2019). *Dialoguri despre educatie si pedagogie*. Ars Docendi.

Rassmusen, M. B., & Wamberg, J. (2010). *Totalitarian art and modernity*. Aarhus University Press.

UNESCO. (2005). *Education for all—The quality imperative*. Retrieved from https://en.unesco.org/gem-report/report/2005/education-all-quality-imperative

UNICEF. (2020). *Our Europe, our rights, our future*. Retrieved from https://www.unicef.org/eu/media/1231/file/Report%20%22Our%20Europe,%20Our%20Rights,%20Our%20Future%22%20.pdf

US Congress. (2018). *National Security Commission on Artificial Intelligence Act of 2018, S. 2806, 115th Congress*. Retrieved from https://www.congress.gov/115/bills/s2806/BILLS-115s2806is.pdf

Varghese, N. V., & Mandal, S. (2021). *Teaching learning and new technologies in higher education*. Springer.

Chapter 3
Artificial Intelligence and the Changing Roles in the Field of Higher Education and Scientific Research

Meriem Rafik

Abstract The university as we know it today is going to die. Indeed, we are now seeing the chaos that precedes any change. The influence of new players, such as artificial intelligence, is incompatible with a university that is an essential element of the contemporary industrial, financial, and ideological apparatus (Deneault in La médiocratie. Lux Editeur, Canada, 2015). The revolution of the academic world is imperative, given that the relations between academia and knowledge reflect the evolution of societies. As a result, we will have to guide innovation, which in itself holds no particular moral value. Innovation is as good as what we decide to do with it. However, the absence of a social project prevents us from creating a transversal policy in the economic, social, and cultural fields. This is why the new university that we are going to invent will allow us to take up the immense challenge of serving us in a world soon to be saturated with artificial intelligence. The objective of this research is to analyze the addition of digital technology to the world of conservative universities and to propose an optimal way of orienting scientific research and higher education represented by professor-researchers, to adapt to a digital future that is certainly approaching. This article is organized into three main sections. The first section will expose the changes in the profession of academic professors in both their informational and financial capacities; the second section will focus on the changes in the profession of researchers, also in their informational and financial capacities; and the last section will offer some suggestions to optimize the profession of researchers and professors in the context of their interaction with artificial intelligence.

Keywords Higher education · Scientific research · Bibliometric analysis · Academic world · Artificial intelligence · Pedagogy

---

M. Rafik (✉)
University Hassan II, Casablanca, Morocco
e-mail: miryame108@gmail.com

F. Roumate (ed.), *Artificial Intelligence in Higher Education and Scientific Research*, Bridging Human and Machine: Future Education with Intelligence,
https://doi.org/10.1007/978-981-19-8641-3_3

3.1 Introduction

Joseph Schumpeter explains in his book *Business Cycles* the notion of creative destruction: Each innovation carries within it the seed of progress. Some major innovations have the power to change the world. Each time they are disseminated, they make it possible to build a new universe, freed from the restrictions of the previous one. A faster, more efficient, and more modern world is generated each time. The whole economic world benefits and the old world disappears, along with its obsolete trades that come to be deemed too slow and too expensive (Schumpeter, 1939).

Most of the sectors that had remained stable until now despite the ongoing changes since the industrial revolution are currently going through a phase of general reshuffling thanks to a new phase in the history of the economy, known as 'cognitive capitalism'. It appeared in the 1990s and is based on the observation that knowledge is increasingly presented as the key issue in value creation and capital accumulation (Dieuaide et al., 2003). As usual, the study and research sector as a key element in this profound evolution has followed all these changes to ensure that this innovation is compatible with human well-being. For example, the industrialization of artificial intelligence (AI) must be accompanied by the democratization of biological intelligence (Alexandre, 2017). To achieve this, it will be necessary to review the education system and implement a strategy that would enable tomorrow's people to face AI on equal terms and cohabit harmoniously with it, and above all to put it at their service in the best way.

This means that the academic world must intervene on the educational level by preparing itself (evolution of the profession of scholars) and by preparing future generations for progress through possible sociological and economic changes. Changes must also happen on the scientific level, enriching both the human brain and artificial intelligence with science in the healthiest manner for each. This will allow us to control our future and thus stop seeing it as a permanent threat.

However, this cannot be done without redefining the objectives of the university, which have gradually moved away from the process of knowing, i.e., discovering one's consciousness and the capabilities of one's mind (Hedges, 2009), along with prioritizing scientific materialism and economism. It should also be taken into consideration that the lack of investment on the part of the state has left the door wide open for other investors who are willing to pay large sums for the credibility of scientists and to take advantage of the educational training market.

The best person to support these changes is the professor-researcher. Concerning one of the big debates of our era 'the evolution of jobs', the profession of scholar may need to change, but will never disappear entirely. Indeed, the surge of artificial intelligence will push human beings to refocus on non-automatic activities (such as coaching, social activities, innovation, or supervision), leaving repetitive operations, calculations, and logic to the machines (Cuillandre, 2020). Nonetheless, this surge will push the scholar into a form of invisible bureaucracy that lies in the 'publish or perish' bibliometric indicators and meta-analyses.

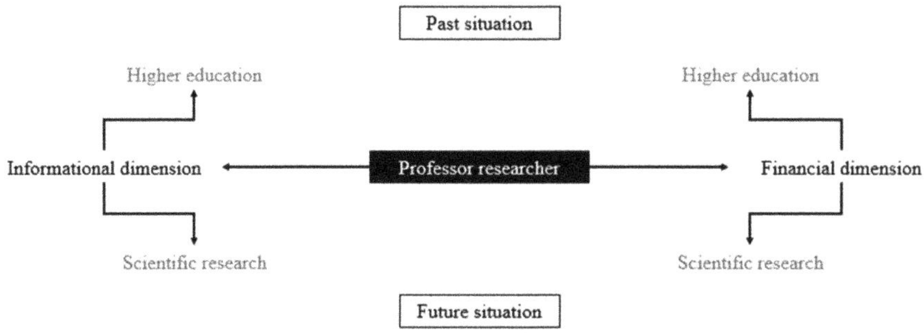

Fig. 3.1 The research structure. *Source* Made by the author

With that in mind, the objective of this research is to analyze the arrival of the digital element to a conservative academic setting and to suggest the optimal way to orient the field of scientific research and higher education represented by the professor-researcher, to adapt to the digital future that is surely upon us. This goal will be accomplished through a futuristic theoretical analysis based on the research structure presented in the diagram (Fig. 3.1), which shows a general overview of the subject.

What is the optimal direction for the profession of professor-researcher to take advantage of technological advancement? To answer this question, this article will follow the following plan. The first part will discuss the changes in the profession of academic professors in both its informational and financial dimensions. The second part will focus on the changes in the profession of researcher, also in its informational and financial dimensions. The final part will make some suggestions for optimizing the profession of professor-researcher through interaction with new technologies.

3.2 Changes in the Informational Dimension of Higher Education

The hot topic in the academic world is the delicate situation in which professors found themselves during the COVID-19 health crisis. They were obliged to resort to a new form of education (distance learning courses), although the method of teaching in the majority of universities had unfortunately not changed since the industrial revolution. On the surface, the problem seems to lie in the use of new technological tools by professors to avoid hindering the continuity of activity in the world. However, on closer observation, this distance learning model has highlighted deeply rooted problems in the education system. The main problem is strategic, the second problem is conservative, the third is pedagogical, and the fourth concerns the emergence of substitutes for the profession of professor, all of which will be explained in the following paragraphs.

Typically, criticisms of higher education focus almost exclusively on issues of accessibility, efficiency, and management, rather than on its mission, organizational structure, or ideological foundations. To a large extent, this is because critics of higher education themselves operate within the modern university and share its underlying philosophy, which emphasizes the triumph of technical perfection over intellectual laziness, along with a transformation (directly for some, and indirectly for others) of the role of teaching from a tool of knowledge and learning to a passport to the labor market. For example, the director of the University of Montreal said so clearly (2011): 'brains must correspond to the needs of companies'. This explains the crisis of 'more degrees for less work' (Deneault, 2015).

Pierre Bourdieu said, 'There are many intellectuals who question the world; there are very few intellectuals who question the intellectual world' (Champagne & Christin, 2004). Our universities reinforce the dominant currents of thought that define our civilization. Moreover, they are conservative institutions that reinforce the established order rather than matrices of change; in other words, the professor-researchers, who are normally the decision-makers, make up for their inadequate financial situation by using their power to avoid going outside their comfort zone. For example, there is a common joke about the academic world's stance on change: 'Reforming a university is as laborious as moving a cemetery—you can't count on the help of those in it!' (Engwall, 2007).

A future doctor cannot learn directly from the patient with a scalpel, so how can university professors who deal with the construction of the human brain fulfill their function without prior pedagogical training? Pedagogy receives too little attention at the university; at least, much less than research. As Bell Hooks argues, 'most of us are not inclined to view the discussion of pedagogy as essential to our academic work and intellectual growth, or the practice of teaching as work that enhances and enriches scholarship' (Hooks, 1994). In truth, the advent of new tools forces us to begin a serious discussion about pedagogy in lecture halls. The students of tomorrow no longer need knowledge—they need the tools to find it on their own. Artificial intelligence favors the self-taught; only in this way will we be able to achieve intellectual democratization.

Additionally, lectures are becoming arduous for both professors and students. In the era of the snapshot where a five-minute-long video can summarize a two-hour-long lesson, the digital dissonance of professors who have never used basic audiovisual equipment is obvious and creates a huge rift that gives the university a retrograde image. The Internet ensures that information is no longer monopolized by teachers. Their importance and usefulness are not in question; this just means that the nature of the need has changed, and they need to adapt to it.

3.3 Changes in the Financial Dimension of Higher Education

The university has been working for many decades to make itself manipulable by anyone who wants to finance it (Deneault, 2015). The predominance of the international financial system over the economy (the World Bank, which encourages the privatization of the education system and limitations on public services) and the instability of this system are two recurring problems that haunt the research and programs developed by universities (Hedges, 2009).

For instance, Kaletsky (2010), in an article analyzing the consequences of the disengagement of the state in the social field, claims that 'the education sector will experience greater competition and strong private sector investment' (Kalestsky, 2010). With neoliberal policies, education becomes a market, and like any market in the capitalist system, it is a site of competition. In the case of universities, competition is one way to balance or increase their budgets (Roc, 2020), a way to compensate for the underfunding by the state. By contrast, private universities have a better information technology (IT) infrastructure and a higher ratio of IT support staff than public universities, which are short on funding. The publisher Marcel Fournier speaks of a 'crisis' in the institution. Far from its original vocation, this institution would now be run by a bureaucracy that appeals only to the criteria of profitability and productivity (Coursin & Jammal, 2020).

The change in the academic world is also linked to another major development of the post-war period: the rise of management, both in professional practice and as a field of study. This trend is closely linked to the emergence of large—often multinational—firms that are run no longer by their owners, but by managers recruited through complex hierarchies (Chandler, 1977). The abundant training provided by universities, MBAs, and business schools transforms students into products that the schools then sell to these private companies and to other institutions that finance them. Today, we witness the rise of professor-entrepreneurs (Deneault, 2015) developing their clientele through cooperation with private companies. This governance of the university does not just make it run amok—it completely corrupts the institution (Mills, 1951).

3.4 Changes in the Informational Dimension of Scientific Research

Technological progress does not necessarily go hand in hand with human progress, but it remains the surest way to achieve it. First of all, scientific discoveries will continue to come mainly from humans for many years to come, contrary to what some prophets advocate based on the entry of artificial intelligence and big data into the world of research, which has caused several upheavals (Véry & Cailluet, 2019). Researchers have been studying the possible development of artificial intelligence and its penetration into the sciences. Their analyses suggest that many facets of the researcher's job should evolve, thanks to data processing software (from writing to publishing), bibliometric tools, and their tyrannies (publish or perish), along with the construction of communities of researchers, meta-analysis, and its impact on research methodology.

Artificial intelligence permeates research, not only as a research subject but also through the practice of data analysis. Artificial intelligence can thus help researchers—without replacing them—in the demanding tasks of production, manipulation, and search for meaning in large sets of documents or data through meta-analysis. This development is increasingly impacting research methodology, privileging qualitative studies over quantitative studies. Once the research has been conducted, it is time to publish it. Several publishing houses offer a set of AI solutions to help journal editors. Various phases of the dissemination process are affected: the initial selection of manuscripts, the identification of reviewers, the verification of non-plagiarism, the review process, and the synthesis of contributions. Some tools even analyze whether the methods and statistics described in an article are accurate (Véry & Cailluet, 2019).

The main advantage of all these tools is saving time, as the publication process is long. Whatever the operation is carried out, the designers of these algorithms and the editors agree that the final decision of rejection, resubmission, or acceptance remains in the hands of the editor. However, a tool that assigns a paper an overall score of acceptability is now available on the market; this could lead some publishers to base their decision entirely on this score, for the sake of convenience. This is important because the number of submissions to journals, particularly the most prestigious ones, has been constantly increasing for several years, and the journal's economic model, partly based on the voluntary work of referees from scientific laboratories, is being called into question (Véry & Cailluet, 2019).

This leads us to the second change—bibliometrics, defined by Alan Pritchard as 'the application of mathematics and statistical methods to books, articles and other means of communication' (Neptune & Mothe, 2015) quantifying written information. Bibliometrics, represented by bibliographic databases such as Scopus (2004), Web of Science (2018, WOS), or Google Scholar (2004, GS), influences each scientific work itself through the number of citations in other works. Furthermore, it influences the researcher's renown and credibility on an international scale through the H or G index, based on the number of publications and citations of the researcher's work by other authors, the language of publication, the pre-eminence of the impact factor of the journals in which the author publishes, and the peer-review process. Peer-recognized publications benefit both the authors and the institutions that employ them; the latter may see their revenues correlated with their researchers' publications.

As a result, this new way of functioning has ended up having an effect of tyranny on publication, summarized by the expression 'publish or perish', which denounces the pressure exerted on professionals in the academic world, especially scientific researchers, through the obligation to publish research results as regularly as possible in scientific journals to advance their careers (Angell, 1986). In particular, this expression mocks the lack of consideration of other aspects of academic work, such as the production of pre-publication or the organization and conduct of teaching. The quantity of publications is considered, in the context of the evaluation, a biased means of measuring academic activity and opportunities for advancement (access to positions, financial support for research projects, increased income, and reputation). This pressure leads researchers to undertake trivial studies that yield rapid results, needlessly reporting the same study over and over again, and listing as authors people with little involvement in the study. This gives the impression that science is in a state of stationary evolution. Thus, productivism and its process of accumulation have taken control and are causing mediocracy to take hold.

The confinement of scientists by institutional economics and the permanent control of scientific work by peers due to the need to belong to a community (a network) induce a form of writing that is not a means of communication or exchange, but of a self-representation that conforms to the standards of the milieu. Academic language is a secret code that some researchers use to show that they are part of the club. Thanks to it, no one can tell whether their ideas are brilliant, bad, or simply mediocre (Deneault, 2015).

3.5 Changes in the Financial Dimension of Scientific Research

Problems related to funding begin with the preparation of the thesis. From the outset, there has been tension between 'modern' (research) universities that create the profile of a future intellectual and polyvalent researcher and the 'older' (more professional) universities that create specialized advisors in a small field. The question of the goal of training at the doctoral level has been controversial since the nineteenth century: Should the university train high-level researchers or professionals? The question is still relevant 150 years later. What has allowed the professional doctorate to survive to this day is financial support from companies, with funding increasingly directed toward sponsored research (Dufort & Hudon, 2020a, 2020b).

Correspondingly, universities have taken the position that it is not their role in society to engage in moral issues. Of course, they seek to operate ethically, but they are committed to the idea that research and teaching require objectivity, which generally requires ethical issues to be disregarded. To understand why these assumptions are not challenged and why universities avoid making moral judgments about the desire for material gain, it is essential to understand the history of the modern university (Ford, 2020).

The modern scholar is different from the scholar of previous decades: Sociological and economic changes require scholars to have a status defined by a comfortable financial situation that enables them to support their reputation and social power, but the insufficient state budgets made available to them oblige them to go down the professional route. Professionalism is socially presented as a tactile contract between, on the one hand, the various producers of knowledge and discourse and, on the other hand, the holders of capital. The former provides and formats, without any spiritual commitment, the practical or theoretical data that the latter need to legitimize themselves (Said, 1996). This situation has proven that there are professions that lose credibility in the collective unconscious when they are associated with non-state money, such as medicine and research. We saw this loss of trust during the global health crisis of 2020, which occurred because we know that the researchers' work is necessarily oriented by the modes of financing (the post-truth era). For this reason, the more successful countries are the countries that have invested in human development, because this closes the door to any possible corruption in scientific research.

This suggests that when bibliometrics interacts with the institutional dimension of the university, a bureaucracy is created based on the researcher's ability to attract investors. The university plays on the researcher's side by telling them: *your identity is an asset and this asset belongs to us* (Deneault, 2015). Indeed, evaluation reports contain sentences such as 'A prolific scientific production with such and such several publications over the last five years', 'A strong international publication', and 'An increase in the number of doctoral students and theses defended'. Research is taking an increasingly important place in these reports, which is not in itself problematic. But it becomes so when excellence in research has become the main criterion for advancement in the profession (Schimanski & Alperin, 2018) and access to opportunities.

3.6 Optimizing the Changes Related to Higher Education

What will be at stake tomorrow often depends on the decisions made today, hence, the importance of considering the long term and thinking about the future in higher education decision-making. The technocratic objective, which is incompatible with the new technologies that prioritize qualitative professions, does not help students either in the development of their critical thinking skills or in their integration into the labor market (Alexandre, 2017).

Surely, higher education is unique in its power to catalyze social mobility, serving to bridge social, economic, racial, and geographic divisions like no other force. As labor markets are constantly evolving, it is clear that the future requires a higher education system that is as dynamic and adaptable as the technologies around which our society is built. The broad outlines of this optimization are already clear. For the first time in centuries, we have a new factor that has entered the education sector, and that is choice. For many years, our education systems have been criticized for presenting the same course in the same way to different students with different abilities and forms of intelligence. However, technological evolution, the health crisis, and the intervention of scientific influencers on the Internet have all made it possible to create the same knowledge using different pedagogical forms, leaving it up to the student to choose the optimal way for them to learn, which will allow the student to advance their critical thinking over time. This is itself proof of their involvement and interest in the teaching output.

However, to create an open scenario for adaptive action, we need to think of the system more as a network for developing collaborative intelligence (Ketele, 2020). This choice is made differently in private and public universities. This can transform their competition into synergy if, for example, one decides to adopt a technocratic ideology, while the other focuses on building the intellect of tomorrow. The labor market does not select its future employee for their public university degree, but for the rigor, they demonstrated by obtaining it, and thus for their perseverance or being autonomous. On the other hand, the graduate of a private university is chosen not for their training, but for the network and experiences they have acquired during their studies; in other words, the choice is made based on the personal qualities of the individual, so that everyone has their place. Wouldn't it be the occasion to reflect on the nature of tomorrow's world, to enter it with more assurance?

On that account, a logical popularization effect is necessary, so that the real issues raised by new technologies become accessible to the greatest number of people (Cuillandre, 2020). It would be possible, for example, to use the techniques of convincing documentaries, and above all to manage the job of a scientific influencer so that it can be framed and cleaned of all misinformation. Also, investing in teacher training and its continuous changes would be beneficial, because frustration with computers will now surely lead them to be marginalized. Digital technology should and will be considered a pedagogical learning tool and will be used throughout the curriculum, especially in distance learning thanks to the massive open online courses (MOOCs), etc.

3.7 Optimizing the Changes Related to Scientific Research

This remark may seem obsolete, but the change that is needed in scientific research today is the separation between the role of the professor and the role of the researcher. This has been an open debate for years. Neither role is related to the other. It is absurd to force a professor to create knowledge if they feel they have nothing relevant to add, and it is even more absurd to ask a researcher to automatically be a good professor. These roles are two professions in their own right, and each requires different qualities. This duality is the main cause of the conflict between work and fulfillment for many professor-researchers.

Consequently, the research field remains one that can provide access to important capital in the academic field. This capital can be counted in publications, grants, conferences, symposia, and outreach. Committed research is no exception to this rule, and researchers who have taken this path will have had to invest much more time in coordination and meetings than their colleagues to meet the same evaluation criteria. Despite this, many have a difficult time trying to promote engaged research at their universities and advance their academic careers (Dufort & Hudon, 2020a, 2020b).

In addition, the development of meta-analyses will require the researcher to acquire new skills in database preparation and programming, as algorithms are frequently unique and developed for a particular use. The researcher will need training in these methods, as well as in building the team with coding specialists and using companies that provide custom programs. It is therefore possible that a divide may emerge between researchers who know how to program and those who do not, the former having privileged access to databases (Véry & Cailluet, 2019).

In turn, artificial intelligence decision-support tools for scientific publishing must also be questioned. They undoubtedly need to be held accountable. Like human editors, systems derived from machine learning are not without selection bias. The case of gender bias is particularly present insofar as the learning machine relies on databases from which the computer will suggest decisions (Véry & Cailluet, 2019). This is because, in past, a vast majority of scientific articles were written by male researchers, which leads to the databases being biased against emerging female researchers' contributions.

3.8 Conclusion

The first question that may arise in regard to this work is: How did an article about the new players in the academic world and scientific research focus so much on research professors? An initial literature review clearly showed that they are the point of convergence of all that we seek to demonstrate, which made them a strategic methodological choice for the structure of this article; secondly, they expose the role of visionaries in the happening of any change. Artificial intelligence, for instance, is a change that is related to individuals, not to organizations. This also explains why the real change of countries that are ahead of the game in terms of new technologies such as the United States or China started with companies, not with a political strategy.

As explained in the introduction of the article, universities should never have decided to leave a comfort zone that has, for decades, perfectly satisfied the individual interests of each and everyone along with the political interests of the countries that promote mediocracy. In post-industrial and dematerialized economies, the evolution of universities is now intimately linked to the noise that can be created by the 'visionary' individuals who can distinguish between real deep social change and ephemeral trends.

Universities are no longer just the repositories of past knowledge; they are the creators of new knowledge and the trainers of a qualified workforce, many of them interacting with many sectors of society. In this framework, the research professor of the future plays the role of a visionary mentor, who moves from the analysis of existing phenomena to a linear dimension of research that creates knowledge in society and politics is inspired, the era of science gathering dust in libraries is over, and in the era of the knowledge-based economy, the main supplier remains the researcher. If science does not yield utility, it loses interest. It is this idea that the publish or perish that is supposedly acclaimed not the research professor who loses value. The research professor has the choice according to these personal devices to choose scientific research or teaching because he is not obliged to be skilled for both, and especially the state has to put at his disposal all the financial resources that will not oblige him to be sold or corrupted. The activism of the twenty-first century is not done in the insufficiency of resources anymore.

In the academic world, the agent of change is the research professor, because they have a certain degree of freedom that can allow them to impose this change or hinder it if it goes against their interests, also thanks to their presence upstream and downstream of thought: their creations and communication with society, either through their scientific work or through their mentoring of students who are the basis of the society of tomorrow. This is for the human and for the machine. Both on the sphere of producing knowledge that will feed the algorithms of Deep Learning in the most healthy way possible and the educational sphere where it will be responsible for the said democratization of human intelligence makes to artificial intelligence.

It is important to take into consideration that the research professor is only the trigger of this change; they will also have to play the role of a political advisor to create a social project that will allow us to welcome artificial intelligence and prepare our societies for it thanks to the training to the professions of the future. The private sector, government, educators, and policymakers must work together to provide multiple pathways for young people seeking to set their first foot in the labor market, as well as to reskill and upgrade workers who are striving to maintain their place in the labor market and will also allow countries to ensure their digital independence.

We understand that this transformation must be rooted in a defined vision of the citizen that the world of tomorrow needs, and we need to build him intellectually.

References

Alexandre, L. (2017). *La guerre des intelligences. Comment l'intelligence artificielle va révolutionner l'éducation.* Editions Jean-Claude Lattès éd. s.n.

Angell, M. (1986). Publish or Perish: A proposal. *The New England Journal of Medicine, 104*(2).

Champagne, P., & Christin, O. (2004). *Pierre Bourdieu. Mouvements d'une pensée.* coll. Philosophie présente.

Chandler, A. D. (1977). *The Visible Hand—The Managerial Revolution in American Business.* Harvard University Press éd. s.l.:s.n.

Coursin, R., & Jammal, N. (2020). Questionner la Société par-delà l'Université. *Possibles*, Automne, pp. 8–15.

Cuillandre, H. (2020). *Après l'intelligence artificielle et la robotisation. Remettre l'humain au coeur du monde.* Maxima.

Deneault, A. (2015). *La médiocratie.* Lux Editeur.

Dieuaide, P., Paulre, B., & Vercellone, C. (2003). Le capitalisme cognitif. Un nouveau système historique d'accumulation. *HAL*, p. 02.

Dufort, P., & Hudon, A. M. (2020a). *N'étions-nous pas des enseignant·e·s ?* (pp. 69–78). Décentrer notre pratique universitaire de la recherche. possibles.

Dufort, P., & Hudon, A. M., (2020b). Sous les pavés, l'université : renouer avec l'innovation collective pour reprendre l'université. *The Innovation Journal: The Public Sector Innovation Journal, 25*(2).
Engwall, L. (2007). Les universités entre l'État et le marché: évolution des modes de gouvernance universitaire en Suède et ailleurs. *Politiques Et Gestion De L'enseignement Supérieur, Issue, 19*, 97–117.
Ford, M. (2020). La remise en question métaphysique de l'université. *Possibles*, Automne, pp. 79–99.
Hedges, C. (2009). *Empire of illusion: The end of literacy and the Triumph of spectacle.* Nation Books.
Hooks, B. (1994). Engaged Pedagogy. Dans: *Teaching to transgress: Education as the Practice of Freedom.* s.l.: Routledge, p. 224.
Kalestsky, A. (2010). «L'État n'a plus les moyens de faire le social». *Courrier International*, pp. 23–29.
Ketele, J.-M. D. (2020). Réformer l'éducation : travailler ensemble au bien commun en développant une intelligence collective. *Revue internationale d'éducation,* pp. 205–233.
Mills, C. W. (1951). *White collar: The American middle classes.* Oxford University Press éd. United States: s.n.
Neptune, N., & Mothe, J. (2015). *ANALYSE BIBLIOMETRIQUE: UNE AIDE POUR L'EVALUATION DES UNITES DE RECHERCHE.* France: Institut de Recherche en Informatique de Toulouse, Université de Toulouse, UMR 5505 CNRS.
Roc, J.-C. (2020). Les universités québécoises à l'image des entreprises. *POSSIBLES*, Automne, pp. 48–52.
Said, E. (1996). *De l'intellectuel et du pouvoir.* essais éd. Seuil.
Schimanski, L. A., & Alperin, J. P. (2018). *«The Evaluation of Scholarship in Academic Promotion and Tenure Processes: Past, Present, and Future».* [En ligne] Available at: https://f1000research.com/articles/7-1605 [Accès le 26 February 2021].
Schumpeter, J. (1939). *Business cycles. A theoretical, historical and statistical analysis.* Didier Lagrange ed. France: s.n.
Véry, P., & Cailluet, L. (2019). Intelligence artificielle et recherche en gestion. *Edhec Business School*, p. 131.

Chapter 4
Traditional and Virtual Universities: The Rise of a Hybrid System

Karim Hamidouche

Abstract During the COVID-19 pandemic and the shutdown measures, many aspects of human life were impacted. The education sector was one of the main fields which were deeply affected. So traditional or classical models of education in general, and especially universities' models, were unable to ensure their missions using the same way and tools. This paper will analyze the rise of a hybrid model of the higher education system, based on the best practices and strongholds that exist within the classical and the new models. University, as we knew it before, the COVID-19 pandemic will no longer be the same. Furthermore, this paper aims to relate how the higher education system across the world has been forced to deeply change its practices, basis, and methodology, by announcing the first draft of a hybrid model, drawing its sources directly from two main existing models, but with different concept and approach. If the future of higher education will be hybrid, the model will be reconsidered in a global way, as well as e new system, including different ways of teaching, using different tools. Some aspects of this change are still unknown, but it is granted that the role of machines (big data, Internet, social media, etc.) will increase, giving the floor to AI to be predominant.

Keywords Higher education · Artificial intelligence · AI · Technology · E-learning · Digital universities · Virtual universities · MOOCs · Distance learning

4.1 Introduction

Change is a global and universal rule. All aspects of human life are conditioned by it. However, various conditions affect the rate of said change.

Nobody can deny that we are witnessing, nowadays, the Fourth Revolution: the era of artificial intelligence (AI) as a new episode of humankind's modern history.

Since the 1950s, at the beginning of AI, deep changes happened: The world where we live was no longer the world of old culture: direct control of humans over

---

K. Hamidouche (✉)
Mohammed V University, Rabat, Morocco
e-mail: karim_hamidouche@um5.ac.ma

F. Roumate (ed.), *Artificial Intelligence in Higher Education and Scientific Research*, Bridging Human and Machine: Future Education with Intelligence,
https://doi.org/10.1007/978-981-19-8641-3_4

machines and technology, which remained "*not intelligent enough to develop their tools.*" In the twenty-first century, humans will be assisted, at least in the current time, by machines that will be able to behave with big autonomy.

These deep changes are affecting our lives at many levels: the way we work, the way we learn, how we do shopping, how we organize our society, etc.

Everything was set in place, ready for the new era to start, and ready to launch the process of crossing next door of our history, according to a long systematic way. However, the coronavirus pandemic, made things happen quickly: Distance working and learning switching modes were accelerated, on a large scale, even within the less prepared systems in the world.

This choice, made by no one, is giving the floor to AI to improve itself as a new basis of the new world: where machines become real actors, not just tools.

Impacted deeply by these changes, higher education is facing the obligation to paradigm-changing: A new model is to be adopted.

In the near past, higher education was based upon two models: classical universities relying on face-to-face learning, and virtual institutions, adopting remote learning tools.

By the end of the current transition, we are seeing, a new model of higher education will impose itself as a dominant hybrid model, conserving the best practices from both ones, and adopting new roles.

In this paper, we will try to explain how the transition from the "old" model we knew of the higher education system, to the new one, was prepared for a long time, but accelerated by the COVID-19 pandemic. This analysis will enumerate the challenges and opportunities, the new model of higher education should deal with.

This paper will describe how higher education systems, reorganize their selves, as a response to the exigencies of the new era of AI.

4.2 The Traditional Model Damaged by the Coronavirus Pandemic

The traditional model of higher education as we know was based on learning face-to-face, attending classical courses, living on campus, spending time with books in libraries, and sitting for exams. This system was deployed on a large scale in the world.

It depended on physical presence in classrooms and on direct contact between teachers and students. To graduate from any college, the use of papers and books (either physical or virtual) was necessary.

Within the digital progress, this model was strengthened by new tools provided by technological innovations. However, the system remained the same.

Anyway, as a direct effect of the COVID-19 pandemic and the major measures taken all over the world in 2020, especially the lockdown, the old model could not resist. The change was sudden and radical, as will be described in the next paragraph.

4.2.1 What Happened?

We can say that the "traditional model" of higher education, based on the (face-to-face) system was not prepared for the lockdown. Mainly because no plans for a massive shift to online teaching were available or ready (Cesco et al., 2021).

The classical system was unable to face the new situation because of its main characteristics and basis. As direct contact was banned and considered dangerous, in the entire world, schools and universities were closed. The education services were provided via virtual platforms and many pieces of software used on laptops and smartphones to gather students and teachers.

Nobody was fully prepared for this high-speed transition. However, some countries could adapt quickly to the new teaching condition thanks to existing alternatives: Teachers and students used too many digital solutions in their schools and universities (digital workspaces, virtual classrooms, etc.).

In most countries, distance learning faced many hindrances to being effective: infrastructure difficulties, technical gaps, and shortage of digital content, to name but a few. The transition encountered several failures in most regions of the world.

Some scholars testify that in the early days of lockdown, spring of 2020, most of us thought it would be for a few weeks or months at most (Boxall, 2020). This new situation, never seen before, is, maybe, the first step in a different era of higher education, based on the main lesson learned from the pandemic: make our systems more resilient.

4.2.2 The Impact of the Pandemic

There had been continuous debate about the future of higher education before the COVID-19 pandemic. It is now taken for granted that the effect of the pandemic will have a long-lasting effect on higher education in general (Blackledge, 2021).

Technology has radically transformed many aspects of higher education systems. Nevertheless, they were not prepared for disruption at such a scale: Many institutions were unable to deliver courses online (Giannini, 2021).

This new experience shows us both the negative and positive sides of the pandemic consequences.

The lost hours of learning, the encountered difficulties, and the decline in the level of the students can be the most obvious negative result of the pandemic. Anyway, it was the reason for many positive changes: The place of digital learning, virtual classrooms, and AI applications was improved. In every country, governments and institutions start making efforts to build their capacities for a transition into a digital learning system.

The most important lesson we learned from the COVID-19 crisis is to adopt a new model of education, based on smart tools, enabling the system to work forever.

All the systems had been reviewed, from the basis of teaching, digital content, and zero paper culture, to the new process of certification and evaluation.

The COVID-19 pandemic has forced the issue and shown that this teaching model is not only possible but also desirable, especially when it comes to cost-effectiveness (Blackledge, 2021).

4.2.3 The Big Change

In the next part of the education system's life all over the world, many ideas are changing, due to many reasons, especially the corona virus pandemic:

- Basis of teaching, tools, and bridges between teachers and students: will not only use the traditional way. This relationship can be effective without direct contact. In the near future, a student can graduate from a college without meeting directly with teachers.
- The digital content basis is going to grow. Distance learning further involves a rich and big basis of digital resources which should cover all topics related to the curriculum of students.
- Zero paper culture: Access to the Internet for students is becoming more relevant and easier, and the consultation of materials is increasing. The adaptation to on-screen reading is also striking, pushing students increasingly closer to zero paper use (Araújo et al., 2020).
- The new model of higher education consists also of a new process of certification and evaluation. Teachers assisted by digital systems can be more objective while evaluating the skills of students and the learning process.

This digitalization process of higher education can be strengthened by an officious Internationalization. A shift from internationalization abroad with its strong focus on a small elite of mobile students, faculty, administrators, and programs toward internationalization at home for all members of the academic community has become more urgent than ever (Altbach, 2020).

4.2.4 Old Model: Limited, but Will Still Endure

It is ambitious, but also realistic to believe that the future of education will be based on digital tools and artificial intelligence (AI). However, according to the reasons mentioned above, the traditional model will not disappear immediately.

With due regard to the gap between developed countries and the rest of the world, and the various policies implemented in every country, the new model will not substitute the old one.

Therefore, the future of education will be multiple. Experts of UNESCO are interested in "The futures of Education."

This plethora of models, even diversified, will have one main common character: an important place of the old model of education basis, which will take place with the new tools, by providing a hybrid system.

If the school did not exist, we would need to invent it (UNESCO, 2021a, 2021b). Schools are considered to be a "central component of larger educational ecosystems" by UNESCO, which consider increasing disruptions—such as the global COVID-19 pandemic, violent conflicts, and climate emergencies—"have made the unique role of schools even more evident." Despite this important status, there is a real need to make a necessary transformation of schools (UNESCO, 2021a, 2021b). It is the pandemic itself that has proved that the school cannot be entirely displaced into virtual spaces.

4.3 The Great Shift to e-Learning Policy and Opportunities for AI

The result of the current change process related to the pandemic will be or can be, as many facts show, a hybrid model of the education system, which will be based on smart and innovative tools, enriched by the latest technologies.

AI technologies are offering a complete solution to contribute to the innovative model of higher education; it can analyze students' learning behavior and performance and provide them with in-time guidance and feedback (Wang et al., 2021). Moreover, they can also integrate students' individual and learning process data, diagnose their learning situations, and assist teachers in adjusting the teaching strategies, which then enhance students' learning effectiveness.

AI has also an impact on all other components of the higher education system such as administration and governance, financial concerns, assessment, and evaluation. We can consider four major areas: the impact of AI on educational quality, the learning and teaching process, assessment, ethics, and future careers (Slimi, 2021).

However, for achieving effectiveness, AI needs several conditions, mainly Internet access, and database development.

4.3.1 The Main Role of the Internet

Internet is becoming one of the most common fundamentals in the life of humankind. All human activities are depending on it, not only to learn but also to manage all the human vital and complementary activities: economy, health care, industry, services, etc.

As for education, research, and innovation, the Internet was confirmed to be the main condition of success. Scholars have more freedom to access data, papers, research works, meetings, and webinars, without going (physically) anywhere.

Internet contributes in saving money, time, and effort. It also provides tools for students and teachers to enhance academic work quality by publishing papers and thesis easily, and checking out for plagiarism, etc., with the Internet, knowledge is becoming more democratic.

AI depends first on the Internet. It is the way of the most known basis of AI: deep learning. Machine learning systems have manifold uses because they can efficiently process large amounts of student data and use it to reach effective decisions (Marcinkowski et al., 2020).

4.3.2 Teachers and Students Becoming Virtual

Despite the hybrid model including classical aspects, physical participation and the presence of students and teachers, in the same place, are not required anymore. At least in some activities, a teacher from anywhere in the world can provide a conference to students from anywhere in the world. More: AI can change this rule.

Education can benefit from Chatbot development. It can improve productivity, communication, learning, efficient teaching assistance, and minimize ambiguity from interaction (Sandu & Gide, 2019).

The AI tools can replace the function of teachers in some cases by giving some answers, evaluating, and helping students in their work.

On another level, the use of technology is affecting internationalization and mobility in a variety of ways. Like "internationalization," "digitalization" is a generic term, covering a broad variety of activities, models, and approaches (Altbach, 2020).

In the same perspective, massive open online courses (MOOCs) can be considered a real revolution in education and learning practices. Courses are offered online, free of charge, and open for everyone, but without credit.

"Students may no longer be limited to conventional classrooms in future schools, but they will continue to need sustained engagement with classmates" (UNESCO, 2021a, 2021b).

4.3.3 Digital Libraries and Resources

One of the most important bases of the hybrid system in education is the digital component. Libraries and resources are becoming digital.

In the current time, any scholar can be able to establish a real academic work, based only on this component.

Digital materials, work, and lessons are becoming easier to reach by all. Thanks to the efforts of the international community during the pandemic time, the database of digital resources was expanded and enriched. Digital libraries and academic databases have increased in number.

Due to pandemic consequences, digital resources and the development of virtual libraries were increased. This offers some important opportunities, especially for students to keep learning while the universities and colleges were closed. But alsoafter the pandemic, documents are permanently and more easily available.

This is why we can consider that the increased availability of a wider range of interim materials in addition to final research outputs, coupled with much stronger recent momentum in favor of open access, places more emphasis on the role of the library as a curator and publisher (Cox, 2021).

4.3.4 A Secondary Learning Tools Enhanced

Before the pandemic, many platforms specialized in digital learning for all. Digital universities or digital education services provided by several universities around the world offer training courses, most of the time free of charge.

MOOCs, virtual classrooms, or virtual libraries, were a real alternative to the classical model. However, it stayed a parallel system, which is considered less credible than the classical one, because of many reasons, especially those related to the effectiveness and evaluation process.

The hybrid model, to be as complete as possible, should integrate this type of learning model, in a way to improve itself, by enhancing these tools, and rethinking the process of verification of identity and the evaluation/certification policy.

Furthermore, MOOCs can bring mobility home and are now recognized by institutions, national governments, and regional entities, for instance, the European Commission, as a valuable alternative to traditional models of mobility (Altbach, 2020).

4.4 A New Hybrid Model or just "Virtual Universities 2.0"?

Major questions arise: Will the new model of Education be new and different from the old one? Or will it be just the next step in the development process of virtual Universities?

4.4.1 History Will not Stop

A logical fact: We had two different models: classical and virtual systems, very different from each other. Now, thanks to some deep digital transformations, as deep as the way that AI is taking to emerge, the new model will be some kind of mixture of both models.

As explained above, the classical model will remain, but differently. The virtual model will be integrated, as the missing part of the old one.

Thanks to the current development, students are now placed at the forefront of a vast array of possibilities and challenges for learning and teaching in higher education (Popenici & Kerr, 2017).

All of these changes may lead to a world in which a set of leaner, nimbler institutions emerge while others disappear. We can imagine that small, tuition-dependent private universities will have a hard time weathering this storm because of financial reasons (Kelly & Columbus., 2020).

4.4.2 The Global Effect

Everything was here; we were just waiting for the Pandemic!

A large-scale problem requires a universal solution…

However, as explained before, change will not follow the same way in every country. Each one will lead its single battle, according to its particular situation.

It seems like a global effect, with particular and individual action, responding to local needs, which are not the same for every country.

The international community is asked to mesh the efforts as well as to coordinate between the solutions provided as singular actions. World efforts should bring a consensus on best practices and ensure the necessary assistance to less developed countries.

4.4.3 AI: New Tools for the Hybrid Model

The hybrid model will be based on AI: This tool will gain increasing importance in the new system: AI is impressive.

It will provide many innovative solutions. For example:

- Chabot's can replace teachers: providing answers, monitoring the evaluation process;
- By assisting teachers: preparing courses, evaluating student profiles, building quizzes;
- Linking bridges between databases and students works;
- Fighting plagiarism;
- Providing advice for orientation.

It must be mentioned that the hybrid system will be different from the two old ones: This is the answer to the question quoted above.

The administration of the future universities will be based on a new structure for the quality of services, the dynamic of time within the university, and the structure of its workforce (Popenici & Kerr, 2017). According to the same author, a supercomputer "*able to provide bespoke feedback at any hour is reducing the need to employ the same number of administrative staff previously serving this function*".

It was confirmed (Aldosa, 2020) that artificial intelligence will affect higher education in two main areas:

1. *Curricula: Artificial intelligence will have a major impact on the curricula in higher education.*
2. *Enrollment: We may see a sharp drop in university enrollment due to the high cost, as higher education is not affordable for many because of that cost.*

4.4.4 How Far Can We Go?

Theoretically speaking, it is clear that this process has no limits. It can deeply transform the university system. However, and for realistic considerations, many facts can be considered as limits, at least provisional:

- The gap in technology: infrastructure, equipment prices; globally, the COVID-19 pandemic has laid bare inequalities that are not only social and economic but also digital (Giannini, 2021);
- The capacity or not to produce enough needed digital resources;
- The quality of training programs for teachers and managers.

While some AI solutions remain dependent on programming, some have an inbuilt capacity to learn patterns and make predictions (Popenici & Kerr, 2017).

Students are facing the challenge of developing critical thinking culture; today, they require more than just information; they require the ability to process the massive amounts of data available via social media platforms such as Google, Twitter, Facebook, blogs, and instant messaging (Le et al., 2022).

The real limits of AI algorithmic solutions in complex endeavors of learning in Higher Education (Popenici & Kerr, 2017) should be taken into consideration. AI cannot do everything. The human role is still needed.

Research on the ethical implications of the current control on developments of AI is important. It is also important to focus further research on the new roles of teachers on new learning pathways for higher degree students, with a new set of graduate attributes, with a focus on imagination, creativity, and innovation; the set of abilities and skills that can hardly be ever replicated by machines (Popenici & Kerr, 2017).

4.5 Conclusion: International Efforts to Make the Transition Succeed

The world after COVID-19 pandemic will not be the same, and new challenges will persist.

More than ever, deeper international cooperation is considered the only response to this crisis—whether to strengthen inclusion, combat inequality, generate innovation, and build the capacity to advance societal well-being and sustainable development (Giannini, 2021).

Current global trends appear to be more radical than in the past and require stronger attention and international cooperation than ever (Blackledge, 2021).

In this perspective, UNESCO launched the "Futures of Education initiative" to encourage a global debate on how education, learning, and, knowledge need to be re-imagined in a world of increasing complexity, uncertainty, and fragility (UNESCO, 2021a, 2021b).

The International Commission on the Futures of Education has created and drafted many reports (International Commission on the Futures of Education—UNESCO, 2021a, 2021b).

It is up to the universities themselves to contribute actively, by leading studies and research, in various fields concerned by this big transformation which was accelerated by the pandemic complications. The number of published studies in the field has increased. However, no large-scale reviews have been conducted to comprehensively investigate the various aspects of this field (Chen et al., 2022).

References

Aldosa, S. (2020). *The future of higher education in the light of artificial intelligence transformations*. https://doi.org/10.5430/ijhe.v9n3p145

Altbach, P. G. (2020). Internationalization in higher education: global trends and recommendations for its future. https://doi.org/10.1080/23322969.2020.1820898. Accessed September 29, 2021.

Araújo, N., Cardoso, L. R., Toubes, D., & Fraiz Brea, J. A. (2020). *Digital competence in Spanish University Education and its use by students*. https://doi.org/10.3390/publications8040047. Accessed September 29, 2021.

Blackledge, J. (2021). Thoughts on the future of higher education in the UK: A personal view with a historical context. https://doi.org/10.3390/educsci11090474. Accessed May 30, 2021.

Boxall, S. (2020). A viral shift in higher education? *Oceanography, 33*(3), 78–79. https://www.jstor.org/stable/26962484

Cesco, S., Zara, V. F., De Toni, A., Lugli, P., Betta, G., Evans, A., & Orzes, G. (2021). *Higher education in the first year of COVID-19: Thoughts and perspectives for the future* (10p). https://doi.org/10.5430/ijhe.v10n3p285. Accessed September 29, 2021.

Chen, X., Zou, D., Xie, H., Cheng, G., & Liu, C. (2022). Two decades of artificial intelligence in education: Contributors, collaborations, research topics, challenges, and future directions. *Educational Technology & Society, 25*(1), 28–47. https://www.jstor.org/stable/48647028

Cox, J. (2021). The higher education environment driving academic library strategy: A political, economic, social and technological (PEST) analysis. *The Journal of Academic Librarianship, 47*(1), 102219 (11p). https://doi.org/10.1016/j.acalib.2020.102219. Accessed May 30, 2022.

Giannini, S. (2021). Stepping up global collaboration to protect higher education's future. In: H. van't Land, A. Corcoran & D. C. Iancu (Eds.), *The promise of higher education*. Springer. https://doi.org/10.1007/978-3-030-67245-4_3. Accessed September 29, 2021.

International Commission on the Futures of Education UNESCO. (2021). Progress update of the International Commission on the Futures of Education (Report).

Kelly, A. P., & Columbus, R. (2020). College in the time of coronavirus: Challenges facing American higher education. American Enterprise Institute. http://www.jstor.org/stable/resrep25358

Le, H. V., Chong, S. L., & Roselind, W. (2022). Critical reading in higher education: A systematic review. *Thinking Skills and Creativity, 44*, 1871. https://doi.org/10.1016/j.tsc.2022.101028

Marcinkowski, F., Kieslich, K., Starke., & Lünich M. (2020). *Implications of AI (un-)fairness in higher education admissions: The effects of perceived AI, (un-)fairness on exit, voice and organizational reputation.* https://doi.org/10.1145/3351095.3372867. Accessed September 29, 2021.

Popenici, S. A. D., & Kerr, S. (2017). Exploring the impact of artificial intelligence on teaching and learning in higher education. *RPTEL, 12*, 22. https://doi.org/10.1186/s41039-017-0062-8

Sandu, N., & Gide, E. (2019). Adoption of AI-Chatbots to enhance student learning experience in higher education in India. In *18th International Conference on Information Technology Based Higher Education and Training (ITHET)* (pp. 1–5). https://doi.org/10.1109/ITHET46829.2019.8937382. Accessed September 29, 2021.

Slimi, Z. (2021). The impact of AI implementation in higher education on educational process future: A systematic review. https://doi.org/10.21203/rs.3.rs-1081043/v1.

UNESCO. (2021a). Reimagining our futures together: a new social contract for education. Report from the International Commission on the Futures of Education (188p). https://unesdoc.unesco.org/ark:/48223/pf0000379707. Accessed May 30, 2022.

UNESCO. (2021b). Release of Progress Update from the International Commission. https://en.unesco.org/futuresofeducation/news/progress-update-release-march. Accessed May 30, 2021b.

Wang, Y., Liu, C., & Tu, Y.-F. (2021). Factors affecting the adoption of AI-based applications in higher education: An analysis of teachers perspectives using structural equation modeling. *Educational Technology & Society, 24*(3), 116–129. https://www.jstor.org/stable/27032860

Chapter 5
Virtual Internationalization at Universities: Opportunities and Challenges

Olga V. Novoselova

Abstract Digitalization, internationalization, and an expansion of flexible distance provision continue to be powerful trends. Scholars have recently conceived concepts such as virtual mobility, globally networked learning, virtual exchange, telecollaboration, and collaborative online international learning (COIL). However, despite the diversity of digital networking, the leading position of most attractive institutions for foreign students still belongs to Universities in USA, England, and Australia. The most important reasons are presumed to lie in the incapacity to appeal to the global target groups and in the quality and intercultural issues of the at-home curriculum. The worldwide situation with COVID-2019 has pushed Universities to strengthen online educational positions and to accelerate the process of viral internationalization in a fight for foreign student recruitment. Due to this fact, the overview of researchers devoted to international marketing of universities, as well as, intercultural components in global curricula is needed. I will explore the existing approaches devoted to describing two drivers and analyze the opportunities and challenges raised in the recent trend of virtual internationalization at universities after the outrage of COVID-2019. Finally, I will give a prognosis of the potential of the proposed concept for future research and practice.

Keywords Universities internationalization · Virtual internationalization · Global curricular · International marketing of universities · Challenges

5.1 Introduction

Expansion of university internationalization in the form of international connections, initiatives, and student movements was launched in the 1980s. This process was related to an increase in research dissemination, students' and scholars' mobility,

---

O. V. Novoselova (✉)
Ural Federal University, Yekaterinburg, Russia
e-mail: novoselova@uralbrand.ru

Corvinus University of Budapest, Budapest, Hungary

F. Roumate (ed.), *Artificial Intelligence in Higher Education and Scientific Research*, Bridging Human and Machine: Future Education with Intelligence,
https://doi.org/10.1007/978-981-19-8641-3_5

and the export of education systems. The international dimension of higher education during this period moved from incidental and personal to organized activities, projects, and programs. It was only in the 1980s that the internationalization of higher education became a more central strategic process. Competitiveness in the international market happened to be a key rationale.

Further profound changes like internationalization occurred due to the globalization of our society and markets. Therefore, universities' performance in the international market was extremely broadened in volume, scope, and complexity during the past two decades. Such activities aimed to improve students' skills and provide cross-cultural comprehension in the form of traditional study-abroad programs, foreign language programs, and getting a degree.

The evolution of various approaches toward a concept of internationalization was launched during that period which could assist in developing a more strategic approach applied by universities. The first one encompassed the "activity approach" with the development of such components as curriculum, student/faculty exchange, technical assistance, and international students. However, the absence of correlation, impact, and benefits evaluation between these activities was not taken into consideration. That is why the further approach was devoted to competence estimation which stresses the development of skills, knowledge, attitudes, and values of students, faculty, and staff. The other two are the ethos approach with the idea of creating a culture or climate that values and supports international/intercultural perspectives and initiatives, and the process approach which has emphasized integration or infusion of an international/intercultural dimension into teaching, research, and service (Qiang, 2003).

Nevertheless, with the evolution of the new knowledge of society based on information technologies, the frames of conventional education and distance have been blurred (Guri-Rosenblit, 2014). Traditional forms of programs tend to be substituted by virtual programs being accessed easily at any destination. Such forms as virtual mobility, globally networked learning, virtual exchange, telecollaboration, and collaborative online international learning (COIL) are gradually being disseminated around the world (Guth, 2013; UNICollaboration, 2014). Virtual transnational education (VTE) and Massive Open Online Courses (MOOCs) are prominent examples of higher education crossing national borders (Knight, 2016, p. 328).

Eventually, the effect of the worldwide situation related to COVID-19 in education has only increased the speed of this evolution and, therefore, obliged countries and universities to improve the digitalization of higher education and join virtual competitiveness.

Therefore, this pandemic situation is twofold. On the one hand, certain educational institutions failed to manage the digitalization process and promptly transform it into a digital platform. On the other hand, the transition to virtual education was sharply accelerated with further obvious necessity in digital innovative activities. This process becomes especially beneficial in the area of internationalization due to dissolving boundaries. More international students will get a chance to participate in various university programs worldwide. Such an opportunity brings a shortage of mobility expenses and contributes to enhancing the level of education.

Thereby, the angle of view to internationalization is being displaced where the question is not just if there are international participants, but rather, if there are internationalized learning environments. (Amirault & Visser, 2010, p. 28). Scholars have distinguished a shift in approach as well toward "internationalization that sees the principal outcome of international education as educating graduates able to live and work in a global society" (de Wit & Hunter, 2015, p. 51). Internationalization, in this vein, involves the facet of encompassing a global component in the curriculum of online distance education which would attract students from all over the world. As well, the way to appeal to global target groups could be modified in quality and intercultural issues, and political factors.

Although higher education internationalization worldwide claims to be international or internationalized, however, institutions do not always match this rhetoric, and the reality is often more a collection of fragmented terms and activities, rather than a comprehensive process and concept. And the urgency of clarification of these guidelines seems to be especially relevant in the period of remote study necessity during COVID. Therefore, the question about the consequences of actions and mainly clear comprehension of notions involved in this process becomes urgent.

5.2 Evolution of the Definition

The process of defining the notion of "internationalization" has been taking place for the last 35 years. The rationale and approaches for universities involved in internationalization efforts have been changing and are still being modified based on the way of modern society transformation.

Due to the expansion of international connections, initiatives, and foreign students' movement, the close attention of scientists to this phenomenon was attracted in the 1980s (de Wit & Merkx, 2012). The basic variant of its definition was produced relying on earlier pieces of work and was described as a process of organizational change, curriculum innovation, staff development, and student mobility to attain excellence in teaching, research, and the other activities which Universities undertake as part of their function (Rudzki, 1992).

However, developmenting this notion clarity, the OECD officially has adopted the definition (de Wit, 2013, p. 214) where internationalization is "a complex of processes whose combined effect, whether planned or not, is to enhance the international dimension of the experience of higher education in universities and similar educational institutions".

From the second half of the 1990s, there was a consistent shift from political to economic meaning for internationalization. The growth of international students' recruitment, their preparation for the global labor market, the attraction of global talents to the knowledge economy, and cross-border delivery of education tend to be distinguished as the significant pillars of higher education over the past decade. The definition was modified again and included not only the broad description of the process but also the dimensions and areas of higher education. Thus, Jane Knight proposed that "internationalization at the national, sector, and institutional levels is defined as the process of integrating an international, intercultural, or global dimension into the purpose, functions, or delivery of postsecondary education" (Knight, 2003b, p. 2).

And recently de Wit & Hunter, (2015) have added some more accuracy by pointing out the intentional character of this process "the intentional process of integrating an international, intercultural or global dimension into the purpose, functions, and delivery of post-secondary education, to enhance the quality of education and research for all students and staff, and to make a meaningful contribution to society" (p. 43). Therefore, this clarification underlines the particularity of strategic activities undertaken by universities to attain the purpose of beneficial internationalization.

Since the late 1990s, when the Internet entailed online delivery of study programs, higher education institutions (HEIs) have been gradually leveraging this innovation and reformulating their strategic directions. Online instruction proved to be convenient for working adults and appreciated by millennials. This encouraged universities to make use of online instruction to enrich course content and attract students (Amemado, 2020). The appearance of virtual learning and Massive Online Open Courseware (MOOCs), foreign branch campuses, and international educational hubs have provided possibilities for those students where physical mobility is not an option. The latter mobility could be achieved through the availability of foreign texts, foreign staff, and links with other institutions via such means as communications technology.

All these innovations contributed to the modification of the definition where "Virtual Internationalization at the national sector, and institutional levels are defined as the process of introducing an international, intercultural, or global dimension into the delivery, purpose or functions of higher education with the help of information and communications technology (ICT)" (Knight, 2003a, 2003b, p. 2).

It is worth mentioning that the general definition concerning the notion of internationalization involves two main components in policies and programs of higher education, they are internationalization abroad and at home which is constantly evolving and becoming increasingly intertwined (Knight, 2008, pp. 22–24). Internationalization abroad constitutes all forms of education across borders including mobility of people, projects, programs, and providers. Whereas, internationalization at home encompasses activities developing international or global understanding and intercultural skills and bears more curriculum-orientated nature (Beelen, 2007).

Thus, this simultaneous evolution occurs in virtual internationalization moderating new forms and proper curriculums. Since any internationalization process involves these components being developed and assessed, the necessity to consider them in the frames of viral internationalization becomes obvious. There is much to be done in defining modern forms of virtual internationalization and their possible transformation as a consequence that occurred during and after the pandemic period of COVID-19, as well as, the global curriculum being applied in these virtual forms.

Purposeful integration of new forms and curriculum requires 'the articulation and assessment of internationalized learning outcomes within the specific context of a discipline which will allow such environments to be used as a means of achieving meaningful international and intercultural learning' (Beelen & Jones, 2015).

5.3 Modern Forms of Virtual Internationalization

Strategic change that happened in 1996 has substituted the focus from delivering information on the learning process. The arrival of new technologies has been slowly changing the higher education landscape for years. But, with the COVID-19 pandemic, institutions around the world are urgently being forced to offer a full package of programs, curricula, activities, and management, which leads to more widespread adoption of online communication and learning platforms. Thus, virtual learning becoming the norm makes educational institutions pinpoint how they append value to students' experience outside of just their academic needs, and this leads to upgrading their technology infrastructure to facilitate new ways of implementation.

Based on the notion that successful internationalization of education is contingent upon activities on three levels: institutional, faculty, and students (Lauridsen & Cozart, 2015), the clarification of virtual forms applied at these levels is required. What should be noticed is the fact that all activities organized on these three levels are strongly cointegrated between each other, and any virtual format of communication entails a specific form and content developed specifically for this format.

Knight (2014) ranges virtual aspects of internationalization into her scaffold of "three generations of cross-border higher education", with the "virtual university" and "online/distance" program mobility figuring in her second generation "program and provider mobility" category" (p. 45).

However, if the spread of online programs is not new and its evolution has been reinforced in various international institutions, the concept of Virtual University seems to be even more interesting in modern circumstances. These virtual universities encompass innovative strategies in restructuring updated organizational structures, collaboration models, delivery modes, policies, assessment and funding models, and skills being acquired by the students, faculty members, and administrators which are going to be the main challenge for Universities. The process of quick transformation and perfect innovative management of all structures involved would entail huge financial expenses and a great mastership.

The emergence of the notion of "virtual university" is considered to appear in the 90s depicting it as "picture a future in which students never meet a lecturer face-to-face in a classroom, never physically visit the on-campus library; in fact, never set foot on the campus or into an institutional lecture-room or learning center" (Cunningham et al., 1998, p. 179). Further, it evolved and this virtual university—a 'university without walls'—is seen as an institution that has torn itself free from the geographical issues of the campus, using the new communications technologies to connect learners, potential learners, teachers, researchers, alumni, employers, research funders, and administrators in a flexible ever-changing network organization (Cornford, 2000). Currently, the term virtual university generally is spread as the form of organized teaching and learning activities over electronic resources mainly over the Internet or a hybrid approach. In that kind of setting the learning environments are providing mechanisms for the learning activities where students' engagement with the learning materials and courses are the main keys (Yengin et al., 2010).

The existence of models of virtual universities could identify the level of digital development in the country and the variety of such strategy implementation. The types of models applied in the development of educational digitalization are defined due to the perspective and the operational decisions of these institutions (Kriger, 2001) or by the number of institutions that participated in the project. Thus, Guri-Rosenblit (2005) has distinguished five major organizational models which are being substituted one by one based on the process of technology evolvement: (1) single-mode distance teaching universities; (2) dual-and mixed-mode universities; (3) extension systems; (4) consortia-type ventures; and (5) new technology-based universities.

One of the first models was the large single-mode distance teaching universities established in the early 1970s, and at present, they are losing their relevance. However, one of the main areas in which distance teaching universities used to surpass was the elaboration of high-quality study materials created by experts and designed to stimulate and improve self-study (Bates, 1995; Daniel, 1996). Whereas dual-mode universities tend to teach on-campus and off-campus students simultaneously, the same admission requirements apply to both categories of students. The underlying idea behind the dual-mode model is that the same curricula can be offered to both on-and off-campus students through appropriate channels of communication. The extension movement of virtual universities is supposed to assist in the propagation of valuable and practical information on a variety of themes among the people by the land-grant universities. The first implementation of this model occurred in American universities where an extension division was launched providing courses for adults in a large variety of subjects (Guri-Rosenblit, 2005).

Consortia-type ventures are another leading model that has emerged over the last decade. Several universities join forces, either within national higher education systems or as an international enterprise, to offer a variety of distance teaching programs. This planned e-University will focus solely on teaching and will carry no research. Instruction will rely on web pages enhanced with hyperlinks, video, sound, and graphics (Beaudoin, 2009; Yengin et al., 2010). The new technology-based universities constitute the most diverse group. It includes all the higher education institutions that are relying more than any of their predecessors on distance teaching delivery through the new ICTs. The new "virtual universities" are delivering their courses through different technologies and are based on diverse organizational infrastructures. Such a model is characterized by the absence of any central campus, and no physical building or classes are supposed to be present. This model is considered to be the future of virtual universities based on worldwide pandemic experience and the growing role of technology-based infrastructure (Rao & Mulloth, 2017).

These forms are not news notions nowadays and initiatives in creating any of these types have already been launched in some ways, but these settings were rare and not successful in the main guideline. The focus was a vague and efficient realization of these projects was limited. However, each university should install activities and studies which would increase the speed of such form implementation to be competitive in the digital era.

Such type of digital educational structures encompasses distinct phenomenon that existed in underdeveloped format to accelerate internationalization. It is the notion of 'international mobility of students which is one of the central and the most palpable feature of higher education internationalization in modern conditions. Due to international borders closure and further absence of clarity on ways to internationalization this issue of other possibilities of engaging students in international activities becomes crucial. Thus, virtual mobility has been identified as an option that could improve this process. It might be treated as "a valuable alternative for physical mobility as it enables students to take part in courses at other universities without having to leave their home university and hence without the financial implications" (Op de Beeck et al., 2007).

Concerning the definition provided by van Wende (1998), virtual mobility has been described as an emerging form of internationalization where students follow courses offered by institutions abroad and interact with students and teachers, libraries, and databases in other countries. Vriens represents it as "a set of ICT-supported activities that realize international collaborative experiences in a context of teaching and/or learning" (cited in Lawton, 2015, p. 77).

Such type of mobility takes roots in European high education research and practice, whereas, in the American context similar practices occur under the term collaborative online international learning (COIL). However, COIL is defined as a teaching and learning paradigm developing cross-cultural awareness across shared multicultural learning environments (Rubin & Guth, 2015, p. 18), while virtual mobility encompasses the significant impetus for creating and implementing digitally mediated teaching and learning formats (Chang & Gomes, 2020). Approaches to virtual mobility include virtual stay abroad or remote access model (a course in another institution), virtual campus model (for join access in resources, joint development of resources, joint activities), joint curricular designs (join design, course adaptation, joint design, and delivery) (Bijnens & Op de Beeck's, 2006). As well, there was various research devoted to parameters used in the categorization of virtual mobility (Pigliapoco & Bogliolo, 2007; Silvio, 2003). It includes collaborative learning in online student communities, virtual seminars, virtual projects, joint thesis work, constructive group learning around wiki-like activities with different stakeholders involved, etc. An international experience by virtual mobility, therefore, is not restricted to one university or country and a group of fellow students. (EADTU, 2010, p. 4). Additional aspects that are less often discussed include virtual internships (Op de Beeck & Van Petegem, 2012; Ruggiero & Boehm, 2016; Vriens & van Petegem, 2011) and virtual field trips (Veletsianos, 2010, p. 290).

Op de Beeck et al. (2008), in the study devoted to virtual mobility tools have defined two categories: synchronous tools which are facilitating communication between users at the same time (for example, chat, videoconferencing, web conferencing, etc.), and a synchronous tools assisting in communication between user independent of time (e-mail, discussion forum, e-portfolio, etc.). Asynchronous communication is the dominant form of educational computer-mediated communication (CMC) (Johnson & Aragon, 2003). Whereas, synchronous communication involves immediate communication between teachers and students, usually in the form of text chat (Johnson, 2006). Some studies report the advantages of asynchronous CMC compared to synchronous CMC and face-to-face courses. They include time-independent access, possibilities for heightened levels of peer interaction, avoidance of undesirable classroom behavior, and support for multiple learning styles (Morse, 2003). Thus, Schwier and Balbar (2002) reported that synchronous communication works well for content that inspires natural debate or passion, but that asynchronous communication may be preferred for content that is dry or requires reflection since synchronous communication may not provide the time or concentration required to engage deep ideas.

However, research on virtual mobility is not the only term spreading around universities as a form of increasing internationalization. Virtual exchange used to be often associated with virtual mobility and online learning; however, it is important to differentiate between virtual mobility and virtual exchange. While virtual exchange refers to the different approaches to online intercultural exchange projects in education, virtual mobility refers to students using online platforms and tools to take courses at a distant university (O'Dowd, 2018).

The Cross-Disciplinary Organization for Telecollaboration and Virtual Exchange in Higher Education called UNICollaboration has designated virtual exchanges as technology-enabled, sustained, people-to-people education programs. They entail the engagement of groups of students in online intercultural exchange, interaction, and collaboration with peers from partner classes in geographically distant locations, under the guidance of educators and/or expert facilitators (UNICollaboration, 2014, p. 1). Therefore, a vast amount of research with various developed terminologies such as telecollaboration, globally networked learning environments, COIL, global virtual teams/communities (Peltier et al., 2003), and online intercultural exchange refer to virtual exchange initiatives.

O'Dowd (2018), the researcher engaged in a study devoted to the implementation of collaborative online learning in university education, has defined some approaches to virtual exchange in higher education. The study elucidates the differentiation of initiatives involved between subject-specific virtual exchanges (development of foreign language competence, intercultural communicative competence, and digital competence), shared syllabus approaches (development of intercultural awareness, critical thinking, and digital literacies), and service-provider approaches (a 'shared syllabus' is developed for the improvement of digital competence and intercultural competence).

The evolution of these forms of virtual internationalization should be systematic which involves not only the design of activities to be implemented but as well the development of the methodological and administrative area at the university. These innovative tools in speeding up the virtual format during the COVID outbreak inevitably contribute to prompt, robust internationalization of the curriculum. And not only internationalization but also digitalization of it is seen to be an emerging topical issue.

5.4 Global Curriculum

Virtual internationalization is generally conceptualized in the main body of studies as a form of curriculum internationalization (CI). Among the first to do so were Blight et al. (1999) contended that "new technologies may allow a virtual internationalization of the form of the curriculum" (p. 27). Schuerholz-Lehr et al. (2007, p. 70) have determined CI as "a process by which international elements are infused into course content, international resources are used in course readings and assignments, and instructional methodologies appropriate to a culturally diverse student population are implemented".

Such definitions are explainable since preparing for virtual mobility sessions, teachers have to look for new curriculum design decisions. In these circumstances, the conflation of synchronic, as well as, synchronic information exchange with intercultural interactions occurs to achieve virtual teaching and learning purposes. In the case of virtual mobility, teachers tend to prepare and realize multilateral international and intercultural rather than bilateral exchanges, participating simultaneously in a virtual process together with students and teachers from several universities. This methodological approach is called the learner-centered approach, with the teacher being a facilitator and acting as one of several resources (Fragouli, 2020; Mittelmeier et al., 2020). However, the presence of the student-centeredness aspect, as well as, self-reflexivity and collaborative learning of students and teachers (co-production of knowledge) is emphasized in some studies (Ehrhardt & Archambault, 2020; Kasenene, 2011).

Although the international learning-teaching process involves both teaching and communication methods (Zelenková & Hanesová, 2019), the major body of literature devoted to the understanding of internationalization of the curriculum in higher education is ranged in the category of student mobility (Fragouli, 2020; Sá & Serpa, 2020). For instance, in the series "Internationalizing the Co-Curriculum", Ward (2015a, 2015b, 2015c) discusses "a wide range of programs and services separate from, but complementary to, the curriculum" (Ward, 2015a, p. 1). Nevertheless, not all of the aspects which Ward categorizes as "co-curricular" range in the category of curriculum, co-curriculum, and learning outcomes in this research. Both the use of ICT to enhance student affairs to meet international students' needs (Ward, 2015a) and the support of international students, their orientation, and integration (Ward, 2015b) range in the category of physical student mobility.

The pivotal focus of researchers in the internationalization of the curriculum relates to the conflation of international, intercultural, and/or global dimensions into the content of it and the learning outcomes, assessment tasks, teaching methods, and support services of a program of study (Bruhn, 2017; Leask, 2015). Though, it is worth mentioning that Soria and Troisi (2014) found in a study of over 80,000 undergraduate students that efforts to internationalize the curriculum at home have had a greater impact on the self-reported global, international, and intercultural competencies of students compared to studying abroad. Therefore, several scientists shed the light in their study on the necessity to acquire multilingual, social attitudes, and intercultural competencies by professors and students participating in the international process (Fragouli, 2020; Sikorskaya, 2017; Zelenková & Hanesová, 2019). The attention to previous curriculum issues cointegration is defined in some recent studies related to digital literacy (Abrosimova, 2020; Mittelmeier et al., 2020) and digitalization (Safonov & Mayakovskaya, 2020) during a modern process of teaching due to pandemic period.

The concept of technology-based curriculum derives from a traditional concept of curriculum, agreeing that curriculum is "coherence and interaction of the main parameters of the teaching/learning process (aims, ways of organizing teaching/learning, teaching aids, and assessment strategy) in the process of continuous improvement" (Teresevičienė et al., 2011). Further studies are necessary to be carried out in identifying a certain methodology and theoretical dispositions which would support the process of designing technology-based curriculum and teaching/learning organization process for international virtual mobility, curriculum design should be based on a certain methodology and theoretical dispositions. Previously it was recommended to base theoretical-methodological dispositions for academic virtual mobility on experiential learning theory (Kolb et al., 2000).

Only some studies are identified where the efficiency of the process seen as a curriculum, and the virtual exchange created opportunities for transformative learning have been shared and evaluated separately (Lauren et al., 2020; Villar-Onrubia & Rajpal, 2016). As a result, an important final caveat is that internationalization is not achieved by only one method or means; virtual exchange should be just one strategy of a diversified portfolio of approaches focused on engaging in global dialog and learning from culturally diverse perspectives within higher education (Lauren et al., 2020). And further research should investigate the suitable approaches and methodologies applied in virtual universities and the form to be delivered by trying to separate notions such as "curriculum" and "virtual mobility/exchange".

5.5 Global Reach

Since the main modification would affect not only the forms or content of virtual internationalization, but also the recruiting process would be contingent upon an innovative environment. Renewed ways to appeal to global target groups would be modified in consistency with technologies, quality, and intercultural issues.

At present, there are two classical online marketing tools employed most commonly in practice. They are e-mail and websites (Krebs, 2006; Meffert et al., 2015) which would not be enough in the new realities to gain competitive advantages. Novel virtual marketing capabilities tend to respond through new processes being faster, more efficient, and less costly which are difficult for competitors to imitate (Vanyushin et al., 2018). Such innovations in university marketing would stimulate global reach and international coverage bringing either opportunities or challenges to institutions (Li et al., 2010). Although increasing literature has emerged recently on marketing and consumer behavior in virtual markets (Blasco-Arcas et al., 2014;

Cheon, 2013; Mazurek, 2012), there are still few studies devoted to virtual marketing in higher education. Nevertheless, higher education marketing has shifted from glossy brochures to social media and the web to acquire prospective students' attention (Sherman, 2014).

Biswas (2020) endeavoring to identify the critical implications of digital marketing for the higher education sector, has concluded that it enables organizations to reach and engage a large untapped section of society, build awareness about brands, and make the potential service seekers as a part of the brand. As well, it fosters customization of the products and services in a cost-effective way using the resources optimally while operating with less lead time.

It is worth mentioning that novel marketing of virtual universities should focus on the increase of applicants' awareness of innovative forms implemented in universities, as well as, on the persuasion of society about the high-quality guarantee of the provided educational services. Thus, marketing would concentrate on the branding of virtual universities, and apprising stakeholders on experiencing getting education in such types of Universities. In the first case, the emphasis would be placed on competitive advantages compared with traditional (pre-digital) universities which are lower costs of studies, and the possibility to combine studying and working. And in the case of informing tasks, the absence of differences between the quality of traditional and digital studies should be delineated.

Existing studies in this area nowadays mainly reply to an approach devoted to using social media to build up brand image and communicate brand-related matters to stakeholders. It is more impactful than traditional broadcasts or messages because people are more willing to read customized information on social media platforms rather than on traditional platforms (Schulze et al., 2015). Likewise, the combination of website ownership application with search engine marketing impact brand image. By using e-marketing, the brand will be easily recognized so that it will increase the possibility of product purchasing transactions by customers (Ridho, 2013). Unfortunately, most research devoted to the marketing of virtual universities focuses mostly on analyzing the platform where the communication is performed to improve the university brand (Biswas, 2020; Sawlani & Susilo, 2020; Usick, 2020), rather than on new forms of delivering this message based on the emergence of the new virtual environment. There are only a few studies unveiling the particularity of communication tools in digital marketing that could be applied in the promotion of virtual universities.

Thus, social media marketing (Peruta & Shields, 2018), virtual fairs, and virtual advising with webinars and online sessions are regarded as hotter topics than older forms of new media. This portfolio includes websites, e-brochures, online events (Kuzmenko, 2020), virtual experiences, social media, apps (Pechenkina, 2017), e-learning with MOOCs, blended learning, and cross-channel marketing, customer-relationship management, and search engine optimization (GATE-Germany, 2016, p. 15).

The diversity of approaches to international recruitment and relationship marketing with virtual means is complemented by OER and MOOCs being regarded as important visibility and recruitment tools (Bischof & von Stuckrad, 2013). Lam et al. (2015) have focused their study on synchronous online recruitment tool applications including live chat and webinars. These tools have been suggested to apply during the early orientation phase and support during the application and admission stages. They identified such advantages as availability of visualized presentation and personalized responses for individual or group questions, easy tracking, relation to the backgrounds of the students and their specific needs, high perceived value for question clarification, as well as, least dependence on good Internet access.

The research devoted to e-brochures posits the priorities of this up-to-date communication tool combining brevity with technology. It offers prospects faster and more engaging ways to get knowledge about the institution. The objective of e-brochures is to generate leads providing access to a blog, program pages, social media platforms, financial aids, and campus recourse, rather than only to a website address, phone number, and mail as it was represented in the old style brochures. Their main advantage is the usage of interactive elements such as pop-ups and quick links to other media channels. Therefore, the direct links save search time if interested parties need further information or want to be forwarded to the application page via the "Apply now" button. E-brochures can also be distributed easily and inexpensively around the world via the university's website, e-mail, and social media. Compared to printed brochures, the university can adapt the content at any time and make the brochures available as often as required. (GATE-Germany, 2016, p. 15).

Loureiro et al. (2020) have affirmed that gamification, specifically, is being used nowadays mainly for educational purposes and market research, with the results of engagement varying among studies. The results of this systematic review reveal that gamification creates levels of engagement and designs the interaction between applicants, especially in the short term. Gottlieb and Bianchi (2017) have examined exhibitors' experiences of participating in virtual trade shows (VTSs). The findings of this study depict that increasing sales revenue, lowering costs, having access to new or different markets, and building brand credibility and organizational legitimacy among visitors who attend VTSs appeared to be the main motivations for participating in these virtual events.

A major trend in marketing is not only the use of various media channels side by side (multi-channel marketing) but also a link between these media channels (cross-channel marketing). In the 2015 cross-channel marketing report, more than two-thirds of the companies surveyed stated that integrating their marketing activities across different channels was a priority for them (Econsultancy, 2015). In cross-channel marketing, the messages are transmitted across all justified channels, for example, on the website, in e-mails, and on social media.

The approach to customer relationship management (CRM) systems represents a possibility of digital relationship maintenance with prospective students. In CRM systems, the information about a registered person and the previous contact with this person is saved. In addition, they offer the option of communicating directly with the registered person (Geib et al., 2006). Originally mainly used by companies, CRM systems also offer a wide range of potentials in university marketing to improve target group approach and save administrative costs (Bose & Sugumaran, 2003; Iriana & Buttle, 2007). Particularly in competition with other universities, the aim here is to provide prospective students with information relevant to them quickly. After entering their data, for example, when registering for the newsletter, prospective students can be addressed specifically via other marketing channels with the help of a CRM system (Khashab et al., 2020). The CRM system is also used to successfully manage the application and approval process. In a 2014 study by the American Association of Collegiate Registrars and Admissions Officers (AACRAO), 56% of the surveyed universities with such a system stated that they use it for recruiting and admission (Selimi et al., 2018) Universities can use it at every step of the communicate application and admission directly with applicants. Some universities even use the CRM system comprehensively, from application and admission to studies and support for alumni.

5.6 Conclusion

The fundamental changes based on contemporary situations affect the way how students learn. It is likely to set the new standard for universities, and it will be the quality, availability, and delivery of virtual content that sets them apart going forward.

However, the term, virtual university, has been overused without paying due attention to its meaning. Many have used the term referring to online courses, i.e., courses offered through the Internet at a distance. Some have used the term referring to online course catalogs, i.e., electronic databases of online courses. The challenges raised due to the COVID-19 pandemic are hampering universities' efforts to shift online and follow not the traditional system of online courses delivery but looking further to virtual universities as the infrastructure for providing students with a learning experience and related support services to complete a degree program partially or online and for providing faculty members with resources for teaching and doing research effectively online.

In this context, the concern is with how new practices can be reconciled with the already existing institutional structure and ethos and how other components will intertwine in this innovative way.

This process is a complex interplay of many variables affecting virtual internationalization which involves the cointegration of curriculum and virtual mobility/exchange. Preparation for international virtual mobility activities requires teachers to develop both socio-cultural and academic curriculum provided for exchange.

Curriculum development in virtual mobility educational contexts requires from Higher Education teachers to think differently when facing paradigms such as the development of a new teaching presence, the design of new curricula, the design of learning materials adapted to different learning environments, the application of different learning strategies and the development of new assessment approaches, models and tools.

This entails the need for further studies which could assist in the development of virtual universities, teaching staff in communicative and social competencies, and academic infrastructures which are fundamental in the novel way of interaction that they establish with foreign students. The upward trend of virtual universities spread is expected to increase in the years which would lead to both cooperation and competition.

References

Abrosimova, G.A. (2020). Digital literacy and digital skills in university study. *International Journal of Higher Education, 9*, 52. Retrieved from: https://eric.ed.gov/?id=EJ1281245

Amemado, D. (2020). COVID-19: An unexpected and unusual driver to online education. *International Higher Education, 102*, Special Issue, 12–14.

Amirault, R. J., & Visser, Y. L. (2010). *The impact of e-learning programs on the internationalization of the university*. Nova Science Publishers.

Bates, A. W. (1995). *Technology, open learning, and distance education*. Routledge.

Beaudoin, M. F. (2009). Consortia—A viable model and medium for distance education in developing countries? *Open Learning: The Journal of Open, Distance and e-Learning, 24*(2), 113–126. https://doi.org/10.1080/02680510902879437

Beelen, J. (2007). *Implementing internationalization at home*. EAIE professional development series for international educators, No. 2. European Association for International Education.

Beelen, J., & Jones, E. (2015). *Redefining internationalization at home*. Bologna Researchers Conference.

Bijnens, H., Op de Beeck, I. (2006, February). Elearning europe.info. Retrieved October 22, 2009, from The Integration of Virtual Mobility in Europe.

Bischof, L., & von Stuckrad, T. (2013). *Die digitale (R)evolution? Chancen und Risiken der DigitalisierungakademischerLehre [The digital revolution? Chances and risks of the digitalization of academic teaching]* (Vol. 174). CHE.

Biswas, S. (2020) Exploring the implications of digital marketing for higher education using intuitionistic fuzzy group decision making approach. *BIMTECH BusinessPerspective (BSP)*, 1–19. 205.147.109.164.

Blasco-Arcas, L., Hernandez-Ortega, B., & Jimenez-Martinez, J. (2014). The online purchase as a context for co-creating experiences. Drivers of and consequences for customer behavior. *Internet Research, 24*(3), 393–412. https://doi.org/10.1108/IntR-02-2013-0023

Blight, D., Davis, D., & Olsen, A. (1999). The internationalization of higher education. In K. Harry (Ed.), *Higher education through open and distance learning* (pp. 15–31). Routledge.

Bose, R., & Sugumaran, V. (2003). Application of knowledge management technology in customer relationship management. *Knowledge and Process Management, 10*, 3–17. https://doi.org/10.1002/kpm.163

Bruhn, E. (2017). Towards a framework for virtual internationalization. *International Journal of E-Learning & Distance Education, 32*(1), 1–9. Retrieved from http://www.ijede.ca/index.php/jde/article/view/1014

Chang, S., & Gomes, C., (2020). *Digital experiences of international students: Challenging assumptions and rethinking engagement internationalization in higher education series*. Routledge.

Cheon, E. (2013). Energizing business transactions in virtual worlds: An empirical study of consumers' purchasing behaviors. *Information Technology and Management, 14*, 315–330. https://doi.org/10.1007/s10799-013-0169-6

Cornford, J. (2000). The virtual university is the university made concrete. *Information and Communication Studies, 3*(4), 508–525. https://doi.org/10.1080/13691180010002314

Cunningham, S., Tapsall, S., Ryan, Y., Stedman, L., Bagdon, K., & Flew, T. (1998), *New media and borderless education: A review of the convergence between global media networks and higher education provision*. Australian Government, Department of Employment, Education,

training and Youth Affairs, Evaluations and Investigations Program, Higher Education Division. Australian Government Publishing Service.
Daniel, J. S. (1996). *The mega-universities and the knowledge media.* Kogan Page.
de Wit, H. (2013). Rethinking the concept of internationalization. In M. Stiasny & T. Gore (Eds.), *Going global: Identifying trends and drivers of international education* (pp. 213–218). Emerald Group Publishing.
de Wit, H., & Hunter, F. (2015). Understanding internationalization of higher education in the European context. In H. de Wit, E. Egron-Polak, L. Howard, & F. Hunter (Eds.), *Internationalization of higher education* (pp. 41–58). https://doi.org/10.2861/444393
de Wit, H., & Merkx, G. (2012). The history of internationalization of higher education. In D. Deardorff, H. de Wit, J. Heyl, & T. Adams (Eds.), *The SAGE handbook of international higher education* (pp. 43–60). SAGE Publications.
EADTU. (2010). *EPICS for virtual Erasmus: New opportunities for international student mobility.* Retrieved from: http://www.epics-ve.eu/images/stories/Documents/Manual_EPIC_EADTU_211010.pdf
Econsultancy. (2015). Cross-Channel Marketing Report 2015. Retrieved from: https://econsultancy.com/reports/cross-channel-marketing-report/
Ehrhardt, D., & Archambault, C. (2020). The gods must be crazy: Students' attitudes and dispositions as enablers and blockers to internationalization. *Journal of Studies in International Education.* https://doi.org/10.1177/1028315320964282
Fragouli, E. (2020). Internationalizing the curriculum. *International Journal of Higher Education, 6*, 18–30. https://doi.org/10.24052/IJHEM/V06N02/ART-2
GATE-Germany. (2016). *Weltweit und virtuell—Praxisbeispieleaus dem digitalenHochschulmarketing [Worldwide and virtual—examples from the practice of digital higher education marketing].* Bertelsmann.
Geib, M., Kolbe, L. M., & Brenner, W. (2006). CRM collaboration in financial services networks: A multi-case analysis. *Journal of Enterprise Information Management, 19*(6), 591–607. https://doi.org/10.1108/17410390610708481
Gottlieb, U., & Bianchi, C. (2017). Virtual trade shows Exhibitors' perspectives on virtual marketing capability requirements. *Electronic Commerce Research and Applications, 21*, 17–26. https://doi.org/10.1016/j.elerap.2016.12.004
Guri-Rosenblit, S. (2005). 'Distance education' and 'e-learning': Not the same thing. *Higher Education, 49*, 467–493. https://doi.org/10.1007/s10734-004-0040-0
Guri-Rosenblit, S. (2014). Distance education systems and institutions. In O. Zawacki-Richter & T. Anderson (Eds.), *Online distance education: Towards a research agenda* (pp. 109–130). AU Press.
Guth, S. (2013). *The COIL institute for globally networked learning in the humanities.* Final report. SUNY COIL Center.
Iriana, R., & Buttle, F. (2007). Strategic, operational, and analytical customer relationship management. *Journal of Relationship Marketing., 5*, 23–42. https://doi.org/10.1300/J366v05n04_03
Johnson, S., & Aragon, S. (2003). An instructional strategy framework for online learning environments. *New Directions for Adults and Continuing Education, 2003*(100), Special Issue: Facilitating Learning in Online Environments, 31–43. https://doi.org/10.1002/ace.117
Johnson, G. (2006). Synchronous and asynchronous text-based CMC in educational contexts: *A review of recent research. Tech Trends, 50*, 46–53. https://doi.org/10.1007/s11528-006-0046-9
Kasenene, E. (2011). Obstacles to the internationalization of higher education in Africa: The case of Uganda, Makerere. *The Journal of Higher Education, 3*, 73–89. https://doi.org/10.4314/majohe.v3i1.7
Khashab, B., Stephen, R., & G., & Rami, M. A. (2020). A framework for customer relationship management strategy orientation support in higher education institutions. *Journal of Strategic Marketing, 28*(3), 246–265. https://doi.org/10.1080/0965254X.2018.1522363

Knight, J. (2003a). Updating the definition of internationalization. *International Higher Education, 33*, 2–3.

Knight, J. (2003b). Internationalization of higher education: Practices and priorities. In *2003b IAU Survey Report. Paris: International Association of Universities*. Available at http://ws4.pucminas.br/imagedb/documento/DOCDSC_NOME_ARQUI20060214115459.pdf

Knight, J. (2008). *Higher education in turmoil. The changing world of internationalization*. SensePublishers.

Knight, J. (2014). Three generations of cross border higher education: New developments, issues and challenges. In B. Streitwieser (Ed.), *Internationalization of higher education and global mobility* (pp. 43–58). SymposiumBooks.

Knight, J. (2016). Meaning, rationales, and tensions in the internationalization of higher education. In S. McGrath & Q. Gu (Eds.), *Routledge handbook of international education and development* (pp. 325–339). Routledge.

Kolb, D. A., Boyatzis, R. E., Mainemelis, Ch. (2000). Experimental learning theory: Previous research and new directions. In R. J. Sternberg & L. F. Zhang (Eds.), *Perspectives on cognitive, learning, and thinking styles*. Lawrence Erlbaum. Internet address http://www.medizin1.klinikum.unierlangen.de/e113/e191/e1223/e1228/e989/inhalt990/erfahrungslernen_2004_ger.pdf22

Krebs, W. (2006). *Marketing der Wissenschaften. Strategien des planbarenErfolges [Science marketing. Strategies for planning success]*. Rhombos-Verlag.

Kriger, J. (2001). Virtual revolution: Trends in the expansion of distance education. *USDLA Journal, 15*(11). Retrieved from: https://www.learntechlib.org/p/93570/

Kuzmenko, G. N. (2020). Event management online: A promising marketing technology to promote a university on the market of education service. *Revista Inclusiones, 7*. Retrieved from: www.revistainclusiones.org/gallery/40%20VOL%207%20NUM%20AMISTADYCOLABORACIONOCTDIC.pdf

Lam, Q., Brenn-White, M., & Böttcher, S. (2015). *Guide to using live chat and webinars to recruit international students*. Retrieved from: http://media.prtl.eu/Recruitment+Guide.pdf

Lauridsen, K. M., & Cozart, S. M. (2015). Teaching and learning in the international classroom: quality principles and lessons learned from the IntlUni project. In *Internationalisation of European Higher Education*. Dr. Josef Raabe Verlags-GmbH.

Lauren, N. D., Garrett, A. S., Townsend, J., & Cathey, J. (2020) Rethinking curriculum internationalization: Virtual exchange as a means to attaining global competencies, developing critical thinking, and experiencing transformative learning. *SCHOOL: A Journal of Leisure Studies and Recreation Education*. https://doi.org/10.1080/1937156X.2020.1760749

Lawton, W. (2015). Digital learning, mobility, and internationalization in European higher education. In H. de Wit, E. Egron-Polak, L. Howard & F. Hunter (Eds.), *Internationalization of Higher Education* (pp. 77–83). European Union.

Leask, B. (2015). *Internationalizing the curriculum*. Routledge.

Li, D. F., Nan, J. X., & Zhang, M. J. (2010). A ranking method of triangular intuitionistic fuzzy numbers and application to decision making. *International Journal of Computational Intelligence Systems, 3*(5), 522–530. https://doi.org/10.1080/18756891.2010.9727719

Loureiro, S. M. C., Bilro, R. G., & Angelino, F. J. d. A. (2020). Virtual reality and gamification in marketing higher education: a review and research agenda. *Spanish Journal of Marketing—ESIC*, Vol. ahead-of-print No. ahead-of-print. https://doi.org/10.1108/SJME-01-2020-0013

Mazurek, G. (2012). Virtualization of marketing. *Contemporary Management Research, 8*(3), 195–204. https://doi.org/10.7903/cmr.11153

Meffert, H., Bruhn, M., & Hadwich, K. (2015). *Dienstleistungsmarketing. Grundlagen, Konzepte, Methoden [Service marketing. Foundations, concepts, methods]* (8th ed.). Springer Gabler.

Mittelmeier, J., Rienties, B., Gunter, A., & Raghuram, P. (2020). Conceptualizing internationalization at a distance: A "third category" of university internationalization. *Journal of Studies in International Education*. https://doi.org/10.1177/1028315320906176

Morse, K. (2003). Does one size fit all? Exploring asynchronous learning in a multicultural environment. *Journal of Asynchronous Learning Networks, 7*, 37–55. Retrieved from: https://eric.ed.gov/?id=EJ1073818

O'Dowd, R. (2018). From telecollaboration to virtual exchange: state-of-the-art and the role of UNICollaboration in moving forward. *Journal of Virtual Exchange, 1*, 1–23. Research-publishing.net. https://doi.org/10.14705/rpnet.2018.jve.1

Op de Beeck, I., Bijnens, H., Michielsens, C., Van Petegem, W. (2007, February). Extending and supporting physical student mobility through virtual mobility. *18th SPACE Conference*, Nicosia (Cyprus). Retrieved October 22, 2009 from http://www.eunis.org/events/congresses/eunis2007/CD/pdf/papers/p121.pdf

Op de Beeck, I., Bijnens, H., & Van Petegem, W. (2008) Home & Away. Coaching exchange students from a distance. A best-practice manual on blended mobility. EuroPACEivzw, Leuven. Retrieved from: https://www.yumpu.com/en/document/read/24137860/home-and-away-coaching-exchange-students-from-a-distance

Op de Beeck, I., & Van Petegem, W. (2012). Virtual mobility: An alternative or complement to physical mobility? *Paper presented at the ERACON 2011*, Athens, Greece. Retrieved from: https://lirias.kuleuven.be/bitstream/123456789/397880/2/Virtual+mobility_paper.pdf

Pechenkina, E. (2017). Developing a typology of mobile apps in higher education: A national case study. *AustralasianJournalofEducationalTechnology, 33*(4). https://doi.org/10.14742/ajet.3228

Peltier, J. W., Drago, W., & Schibrowsky, J. A. (2003). Virtual communities and the assessment of online marketing education. *Journal of Marketing Education, 25*(3), 260–276. https://doi.org/10.1177/0273475303257762

Peruta, A. & Shields, A.B. (2018). Marketing your university on social media: a content analysis of Facebook post types and formats. *Journal of Marketing for Higher Education, 28*(2), 175–191. https://doi.org/10.1080/08841241.2018.1442896.

Pigliapoco, E., & Bogliolo, A. (2007, November). Accessible virtual mobility. *EADTU's 20th Anniversary Conference "International courses and services online: Virtual Erasmus and a new generation of Open Educational Resources for a European and global outreach*" Retrieved from: http://www.eadtu.nl/conference-2007/files/I6.pdf

Qiang, Z. (2003). Internationalization of higher education: Towards a conceptual framework. *Policy Futures in Education, 1*(2), 248–270. https://doi.org/10.2304/pfie.2003.1.2.5

Rao, B., & Mulloth, B. (2017). The role of universities in encouraging growth of technology-based new ventures. *International Journal of Innovation and Technology Management, 14*(04), 1750014. https://doi.org/10.1142/S0219877017500146

Ridho, M. R. (2013). Pengaruh E-Marketing Terhadap Citra Merek Nay@ Dam PadaPtKreasi Putra Serayu. *Computer Based Information System Journal*, [S.l.], v. 1, n. 1, mar. 2013. ISSN 2621-5292. Retrieved from: http://113.212.163.133/index.php/cbis/article/view/347

Rubin, J., & Guth, S. (2015). Collaborative online international learning: An emerging format for internationalizing curricula. In A. S. Moore & S. Simon (Eds.), *Globally networked teaching in the humanities: Theories and practices* (pp. 15–27). Routledge.

Rudzki, R. (1992, November). The Internationalization of Faculty Activities. Paper delivered at the Annual Conference of the Council on International Educational Exchange (CIIEE), Berlin.

Ruggiero, D., & Boehm, J. (2016). Design and development of a learning design virtual internship program. *International Review of Research in Open and Distance Learning, 17*(4), 105–120. https://doi.org/10.19173/irrodl.v17i4.2385

Sá, M. J., & Serpa, S. (2020). Cultural dimension in internationalization of the curriculum in higher education. *Education Sciences, 10*(12), 375. https://doi.org/10.3390/educsci10120375

Safonov, A. S., & Mayakovskaya, A. V. (2020). Post-digital world, pandemic, and higher education. *International Journal of Higher Education, 9*, 90–94. Retrieved from: https://eric.ed.gov/?id=EJ1281240

Sawlani, D. K., & Susilo, D., (2020). How digital marketing helps higher education institutions branding. *International Journal of Multidisciplinary Educational Research, 9*, 5(3), 45–55.

Schuerholz-Lehr, S., Caws, C., Van Gyn, G., & Preece, A. (2007). Internationalizing the higher education curriculum: An emerging model for transforming faculty perspectives. *Canadian Journal of Higher Education, 37*(1), 67–94. Retrieved from: https://eric.ed.gov/?id=EJ771047

Schulze, C., Scholer, L., & Skiera, B. (2015). Customizing social media marketing. *MIT Sloan Management Review, 56*(2), 8. Retrieved from: https://sloanreview.mit.edu/wp-content/uploads/2014/11/04a35a22a1.pdf

Schwier, R. A., & Balbar, S. (2002). The interplay of content and community in synchronous and asynchronous communication: Virtual communication in a graduate seminar. *La Revue Canadienne De L'apprentissage Et De La Technologie [Canadian Journal of Learning and Technology]*, 28. Retrieved from: https://www.learntechlib.org/p/43162/

Selimi, N., Trpkovska, M. A., Bexheti, L. A., & Fetaji, M. (2018). Utilization of customer relationship management (CRM) theory, prototype, and tools for improved strategic marketing in HE. In *2018 7th Mediterranean Conference on Embedded Computing (MECO)*, Budva, Montenegro, pp. 1–4, https://doi.org/10.1109/MECO.2018.8405992

Sherman, R. (2014), *Proving the value of digital marketing in higher education.* OHO Interactive. Retrieved from https://www.oho.com/blog/provingvalue-digital-marketing-best-practicesguide-now-available

Sikorskaya, I. (2017). Internationalization of higher education: Intercultural dimension. *Innovative Solution in Modern Science, 8*, 36. Retrieved from: https://naukajournal.org/index.php/ISMSD/article/view/3

Silvio, J. (2003). Global learning and virtual mobility. Retrieved from: http://www.friends-partners.org/utsumi/Global_University/Global%20University%20System/UNESCO_Chair_Book/Manuscripts/Part_IV_Global_Collaboration/Silvio,%20Jose/Silvio_web/SilvioD9.htm

Soria, K. M., & Troisi, J. (2014). Internationalization at home alternatives to study abroad: Implications for students' development of global, international, and intercultural competencies. *Journal of Studies in International Education., 18*(3), 261–280. https://doi.org/10.1177/1028315313496572

Teresevičienė, T., Volungevičienė, A., & Daukšienė, E. (2011). *Virtual mobility for teachers and students in higher education. Comparative research study on virtual mobility.* Kaunas. Retrieved from: https://hdl.handle.net/20.500.12259/36767

UNICollaboration. (2014). Position paper: Virtual exchange in the European Higher Education Area. Retrieved from http://uni-collaboration.eu/sites/default/files/Positionpaper_1.pdf

Usick, S. P. (2020). Digital marketing as a factor of competitiveness of a modern University. *Labour and Social Relations., 31*(1), 123–131. https://doi.org/10.20410/2073781520203111123131

Vanyushin, V., Bengtsson, M., Nesholm, M., et al. (2018). International cooperation on innovation: Is the benefit worth the challenges? *Review of Managerial Science, 12*, 535–557. https://doi.org/10.1007/s11846-017-0272-x

van der Wende, M. (1998). *Virtual mobility: New technologies and the internationalization of higher education.* NUFFIC.

Veletsianos, G. (Ed.). (2010). *Emerging technologies in distance education.* AU Press.

Villar-Onrubia, D., & Rajpal, B. (2016). Online international learning: Internationalising the curriculum through virtual mobility at Coventry University. *Perspectives: Policy and Practice in Higher Education, 20*(2–3), 75–82. https://doi.org/10.1080/13603108.2015.1067652

Vriens, M., & van Petegem, W. (2011). Make it work! Integrating virtual mobility in international work placements. Retrieved from http://www.euvip.eu/resources/Manual_ONLINE.pdf

Vriens, M. (2010). Virtual mobility: An alternative or complement to physical mobility. Retrieved from www.iated.org/presentations/pv_11080.pptx

Ward, H. (2015a). *Internationalizing the co-curriculum. Part one: Integrating international students.* ACE.

Ward, H. (2015b). *Internationalizing the co-curriculum. Part three: Internationalization and student affairs.* ACE.

Ward, H. (2015c). *Internationalizing the co-curriculum. Part two: Global and intercultural education in the co-curriculum.* ACE.

Yengin, I., Karahoca, D., Karahoca, A., & Uzunboylu, H. (2010). Re-thinking virtual universities. *Procedia—Social and Behavioral Sciences, 2*, 5769–5774. https://doi.org/10.1016/j.sbspro.2010.03.941

Zelenková, A., & Hanesová, D. (2019). Intercultural competence of university teachers: A challenge of internationalization. *Journal of Language and Cultural, 7*, 1–18. https://doi.org/10.2478/jolace-2019-0001

Chapter 6
Transformations of the Scientific and Technological Revolution and the Role of AI for Education Systems in the Sustainable Development Paradigm

Viktor Zinchenko

Abstract This paper aims to consider the human dimension of education for the sustainable development of society. A systematic approach to value analysis of social institutions should be used as a research methodology. The education for sustainable development should be based on the latest technical achievements, but these achievements themselves are not an end in themselves. The goal of this education is the development of humans as a person and humanity as a species in the face of increasing technological and other threats to the very existence of mankind. At the same time, technologies turn out to be ambivalent—they can serve both the destruction of mankind and a significant deterioration in the conditions of its existence, or the development of mankind and the improvement of these conditions. Artificial intelligence (AI) is a prime example. AI could be used as a resource for education, but only until AI itself began to use people receiving education as its resource.

Keywords Education for sustainable development · Artificial intelligence · Digitalization · Risks · Values · Global institutional transformations · Internationalization of higher education and science · Research activities · Stages of globalization · Science · Educational institutions

6.1 Introduction

The place of the country in the modern world today is more determined by the quality of human capital, the state of education, and the degree of use of science and technology in production.

In addition to certain realities of globalization, and institutional transformations for the sustainable development of society in the context of the internationalization

V. Zinchenko (✉)
Department of University Research Activities, Institute of Higher Education, National Academy of Educational Sciences of Ukraine, Kyiv, Ukraine
e-mail: vvzinchenko@ukr.net

F. Roumate (ed.), *Artificial Intelligence in Higher Education and Scientific Research*, Bridging Human and Machine: Future Education with Intelligence,
https://doi.org/10.1007/978-981-19-8641-3_6

of higher education and science, there are also equally real trends in the world of regionalization, dissociation, and even de-socialization.

Institutionalized civil society is a socio-cultural factor, which includes the attitude of the person to the means not only of material production but also of one's self-production as a social, cultural being.

The decision on the degree of participation or limitation of AI in modern education should be theoretically grounded by researchers and technically prepared by programmers and other AI practitioners, but in addition, such a decision should be discussed and agreed upon with the participation of the common public. The risks of such a decision should be calculated by professionals, but the final decision can only be made on a democratic basis and take into account liberal and social values.

It is necessary to investigate the transformational models of globalized world development and institutional transformations for sustainable development of society in the context of the internationalization of higher education and science.

6.2 Methods

The rapid gradual globalization is facilitated by the rapid development of information and communication technologies and the idea of a network-based way of organizing social activity. It should be applied integrative philosophical conceptualization and scientific synthesis of existing concepts and theories of the relevant direction.

6.3 Results and Discussion

The process of education, teaching, and acquiring knowledge takes place in society, concentrating on its scientific and technological spheres.

Analyzing the global and large-scale trends is essential for decision-making that will ensure the construction of a sustainable environment and future-ready ecological education.

In its 2019 report, the OECD cites two megatrends affecting the future of education: globalization and digitalization. In OECD countries, it is predicted that this will affect higher education systems at first, as they will have to work harder to attract the best students in a much more mobile and competitive market.

In many countries, adults have inadequate complex digital information management skills, therefore, governments and employers must seriously address issues relating to not only the continuity of education but also its comprehensiveness.

Robotics and intelligent systems are rapidly evolving directly now, especially today when it brings substantial benefit (and possibly—some dangers and damage), and now they significantly define our being—and it will soon be even more essential to determine. The robots are becoming more and more like a human, and a person learns to interact with them, constantly improving them not only externally, but also internally.

In Japan robot—android Pepper—was officially accepted into high school in the city of Waseda. Pepper learns with children, who receive a unique chance to interact with a robot (Hooper, 2018). Scientists and educators believe that such communication will be useful to them in their future life. According to the developers, the robot is equipped with a large number of cameras and sensors that allow it to recognize and respond to almost the entire spectrum of human emotions: joy, sadness, fear, excitement, and irritation. He also can teach himself.

Earlier in Japan, for the first time in history, a cybernetic android named NAO joined the staff of the largest of the banks Tokyo Mitsubishi UFJ bank (McCurry, 2015). The NAO is a humanoid robot developed by Soft Bank Corporation of information technology. NAOs are easy to move and gesture with manipulators, with the help of cameras and sound sensors, they react to visitors, answer questions, and can keep thematically diverse conversations in many languages.

Modern social designers should pay special attention to the latest technological trends in innovation and be able to predict the future. And for this, first of all, many scientists recommend reading science fiction, since this literature stimulates brain activity, and develops imagination and thinking.

It is no coincidence that science fiction is very popular in China. Neil Gaiman said in an interview for The Guardian that the Chinese interest in science fiction is since they were brilliant and good at imitating, but was bad with innovation, and inventions and had problems with imagination in the field of innovation (Gaiman, 2013).

As a result, the Chinese sent their representatives to the US—to Apple, Microsoft, Google, etc.—and asked the people who invent the future to tell about themselves. As a result, it turned out that they all read science fiction when they were children. The focus on solid science fiction in China correlates very well with the victories of Chinese students in international science tests and competitions.

It turns out that the Chinese are actively beginning to shape their image of the future, desired positive future.

Fear of artificial intelligence (AI) was born in 1960-s Irvin John Good, a British mathematician, cryptographer, and cryptographer worked with Alan Turing on breaking the German cipher machine "Enigma" during the Second World War.

Good's reflections on AI led him to the idea of a super-intelligent machine, which, through self-learning, was able to surpass the intellect of a person, no matter how smart he would be. When this machine begins to build machines similar to itself, an "intellectual explosion" will occur—this will be the last invention that a person needed to make (Good, 1965).

But if supramental machine once understands that a human she did not need anymore and will behave like Terminator—to restrict the rights of people and possibly kill them?

Not surprisingly, Good's ideas are now back on track. Is it surprising that they were picked up by leading representatives of science and the IT industry?

"The development of full artificial intelligence can bring the decline of the human era closer"—said the famous physicist Stephen Hawking in 2014 (Cellan-Jones, 2014).

"At first, machines that are not burdened with intelligence will do most of the work for us. And it's good if we learn to manage them correctly. But after a few decades, the AI will develop to such a degree to become a cause for concern"—echoes the founder of «Microsoft» Bill Gates (Holley, 2015).

The head of "Tesla" Elon Musk went further, donated $7 million for research on AI security "Future Life Institute" and compared the AI developers to the armed with holy water exorcists who are trying to tame a demon (Suciu, 2015).

Since the 1960s, when it began to develop as a branch of science and education, "engineering psychology and pedagogy" had explored the processes and means of information exchange between humans and machines, as well as technical means of automation and their form and between models of communication themselves.

Ideas and ethical conflicts in this area inspire, in particular, the directions for possible behavioral calculations of the android technology industry, innovations in robotics, the field of artificial intelligence, and the digitalization of education.

The system of education is yet largely behind the trends and processes of digitalization and therefore more efforts are needed to take advantage of the tools and strengths of the new technologies, while addressing concerns regarding potential abuse, such as unauthorized cybernetic invasion and privacy issues (Sintschenko, 2017).

The educational system and institutions should also take into account the fact that the need for digital literacy and critical thinking is growing not only among young students but also among people of the older generations. One of the frames for education development is the European strategy for sustainable development. This strategy is coherent with the Resolution of the United Nations General Assembly "*Transforming our world: the 2030 Agenda for Sustainable Development*" that formulates Sustainable Development Goals (SDGs) that target key areas for implementing this global comprehensive multi-level strategy for social, governmental, and institutional sustainable development (Vereinte Nationen, 2015).

Accordingly, the education system and educational institutions should be developed, transformed, and improved as institutions that should create and strengthen a safe, non-violent, inclusive, and effective learning environment for all members of society. Which, in the end, will help to achieve success in cooperation at all levels—both in education and science and in society as a whole.

All these official documents need to be filled with the idea of readiness to fend off threats from AI. Such ideas of the "existential threat" from AI to humans were publicly expressed by Stephen Hawking, Bill Gates, Steve Wozniak, Jack Ma, Elon Musk, and other scientists and "captains" of international business (Kohli, 2015). One of the most radical speakers on this topic is the head of Tesla and SpaceX, American businessman and billionaire Elon Musk who declared the threat to humanity from AI.

Musk noted: "We should be concerned about where AI is going. The people I see being the most wrong about AI are the ones who are very smart because they can't imagine that a computer could be way smarter than them. That's the flaw in their logic. They're just way dumber than they think they are" (Matousek, 2020). The speed with which all AI algorithms are improving is gaining momentum, and technology is faster than people think, says Elon Musk.

Musk believes that artificial intelligence is a dangerous technology for humanity, capable of destabilizing the situation around the world.

This is not the first time Musk has spoken about the dangers of AI for humanity. Since 2016, he has warned that a person can become a pet for intelligent machines that have seized power. And has since regularly called for regulation of AI technology. He once co-founded OpenAI, a nonprofit organization that tries "to be the first to create AGI—a machine with the learning and reasoning powers of a human mind" (Hao, 2020). Later Musk stepped back from the leadership of this company, with a Twitter comment "I have no control & only very limited insight into OpenAI. Confidence in Dario for safety is not high" (Musk, 2020). This Musk's demarche was his specific reaction to a program review of OpenAI crew (and Dario Amodei as its research director) ambitions (Hao, 2020). There is no doubt that "By extrapolation, AGI could be catastrophic without the careful guidance of a benevolent shepherd", but it seems certain that many other similar companies do not agree that "OpenAI wants to be that shepherd" (Hao, 2020).

However, among all AI developers, Musk is most concerned about Deep Mind—a division of Google. "Just the nature of the A.I. that they're building crushes all humans at all games," said the head of Tesla in an interview for the New York Times. "I mean, it's the plotline in 'War Games'" (Dowd, 2020). In this Cold War film, a teenage hacker connects to a government supercomputer run by AI and trained in war simulators. During the game, AI convinces the authorities that a nuclear attack is inevitable. Comparing the algorithms of Deep Mind with the War Games, Musk claims that in the next five years, AI will surpass a person in intelligence and we probably will not even notice it.

"We're headed toward a situation where A.I. is vastly smarter than humans and I think that time frame is less than five years from now. But that doesn't mean that everything goes to hell in five years. It just means that things get unstable or weird" (Dowd, 2020) and he also said: "Nobody would suggest we allow the world to just build nuclear warheads if they want that would be insane. And mark my words: AI is far more dangerous than nukes" (Matousek, 2020). It seems Musk wants to be the first again—but only as a winner, not as a loser: he doesn't want to be responsible in case of a harmful effect of new AI activity on humans.

At one time, Isaac Asimov predicted the need to regulate the relationship between humans and creatures created by them (androids, robots, cyborgs, clones, sigmoids, etc.), and formulated the "Three Laws of Robotics":

(1) "A robot may not injure a human being or, through inaction, allow a human being to come to harm.
(2) A robot must obey the orders given to it by human beings except where such orders would conflict with the First Law.

(3) A robot must protect its existence as long as such protection does not conflict with the First or Second Laws" (Asimov, 1950).

But in the very close future, it is quite possible that because of the bad ecology, and poor genetic ability of mankind, but its high technical abilities and its sophisticated medicine it will be almost no "pure" humans, but predominantly cyber creatures and AI bearers. There comes a time when above mentioned three laws must be at least supplemented with the following forth law (B.Stern. "Human is a… (Necessary addition to the three laws of Asimov)"): "An intelligent being cannot harm another intelligent being or, by his inaction, allow another intelligent being to be harmed" (Stern, 1983, p. 90).

From this point of view era of post-humanism has almost come. But probably it is possible to find an answer to the question of limits for Homo Sapiens inside itself Homo Sapiens investigations. "Modern mankind is potentially partly related to the subspecies of Homo Sapientissimus. For this reason, the highest values of the 'Man of Truly Reasonable' gradually become the results of mental functions (thinking, consciousness, reason), more precisely, formulated and implemented ideas based on the content of the stage worldview, as well as on the principles of morality and types of activity corresponding to it (including economic activity)". The subspecies of "Proper Homo Sapiens" begin to differ not in morphological features, but in the mega-structure of connections between the neurons of the brain, as well as in the content of essential and status needs, goods and values that corresponds to this mega-construction (Lindblad, 1991, pp. 228–230). It could be done with additional technology like Musk's Neuralink as well as with evolutionary changes in human being and their mind. Such changes should be prepared with help of the correct educational strategy.

Education should orient on constructivism as a worldview. It is wrong to wait for new unexpected problems—humans should make solutions to problems by creating their problems (Zinchenko, 2021), and due to the forming of their activities based on their reasoning and deliberation of their predictable future.

6.4 Conclusion

The preparation of the next generation to participate in the sustainable development of society as the goal of modern education does not have an unambiguous correlation with the digitalization of education in general and the introduction of artificial intelligence in education in particular. AI should partly enter as a component of education, and part should remain outside of it. The digitalization of the education system is taking place all over the world almost uncontrollably by civil society and without taking into account all the strategic risks. The problem of risks is raised not by government officials and scientists but mainly by public figures and private company representatives. It could appear a false impression that only representatives of the technical elites or special services of states can solve such issues. Although, at least in the field of education, the decision on digitalization and its degree should be made with the obligatory participation of all citizens of the state, especially the parents of students. This is a concrete answer to the demand for the preservation of democratic and liberal values based on education in modern society.

When universities state that it is worth paying significant attention to 4IR, it means that they can no longer rely on traditional forms of human thinking and imagination. But they need a mindset that depends on the algorithmic operations of machine technologies. In this sense, 4IR has changed not only what we do and how we do it, but also who we are or, more precisely, who we have become. In particular, analyzing this problem, emphasize that the point is not that machines have replaced man, but that people have become embodied in machines. And it is no longer important what biological, synthetic, organosilicon, natural, or artificial origin will have new species that will claim to join the human race. But in this case, the title and status of "Human" will require even more correspondence and evidence-based affiliation than today, when it is automatically assigned to all representatives of the biological species "Homo Sapiens" (even those quasi-human beings who are guided solely by instinctive goals and needs of reflexes). The secondary nature of names is precise what name to give to a phenomenon, and not its semantic essence. That is why we need to think carefully about the prospects for the development of forced distance education triggered by the pandemic since our main task today is to preserve inter-human relations. In the context of a global pandemic and the approaching prospect of achieving a "technological singularity", we need new knowledge and skills, including in the use of technologies and ideas to work effectively with them. Also, taking into account the importance of the growing "human factor", purely humanistic dimensions come to the fore when determining higher education strategies for the sustainable development of modern societies. In particular, an important practical mechanism for achieving effective results in the implementation of the sustainable development strategy is to maximize opportunities for free, inclusive, fair, and high-quality completed primary, secondary, and higher education for all members of the human race, which will require us to re-evaluate existing socio-economic strategies both on a national and global scale. In our opinion, the mission of universities of the XXI century is to form a developed personality, a person of a high cultural level who can act in situations that are characterized by significant risks-economic, environmental, political, etc. A university graduate who can implement successful life activities in such conditions and act as a subject for implementing sustainable development goals should possess not only, and not so much, individual professional competencies, but such general qualities as the ability to solve complex problems, have critical, independent, and original thinking, as well as the ability to generate new knowledge and act in a situation of uncertainty, when implicit knowledge and skills, as well as any ready-made instructions, are either absent or ineffective. That is why higher education can and should form a cultural personality and a citizen of a global society that can effectively act in the conditions of the XXI century, which are characterized by uncertainty and risk. To do this, all levels, models, and systems of education must be transformed to develop human intelligence on a global scale through the introduction of new educational strategies and their implementation based on shared values that future professionals share and follow, both in their professional activities and in their daily lives.

References

Asimov, I. (1950). *I, Robot* (p. 253). Gnome Press.

Cellan-Jones, R. (2014). *Stephen Hawking warns artificial intelligence could end mankind*. Retrieved from: https://www.bbc.com/news/technology-30290540

Dowd, M. (2020). Elon Musk, blasting off in domestic bliss. *New York Times*. July 25, 2020. Retrieved from: https://www.nytimes.com/2020/07/25/style/elon-musk-maureen-dowd.html

Gaiman, N. (2013). Why our future depends on libraries, reading, and daydreaming. Retrieved from: https://www.theguardian.com/books/2013/oct/15/neil-gaiman-future-libraries-reading-daydreaming

Good, I. J. (1965). Speculations concerning the first ultraintelligent machine. Retrieved from: https://purl.stanford.edu/gz727rg3869

Hao, K. (2020). The messy, secretive reality behind OpenAI's bid to save the world. *MIT Technological Review*. February 17, 2020. Retrieved from: https://www.technologyreview.com/2020/02/17/844721/ai-openai-moonshot-elon-musk-sam-altman-greg-brockman-messy-secretive-reality/

Hooper, R. (2018). Get ready for the robot invasion—of our classrooms. *The Japan Times*. Retrieved from: https://www.japantimes.co.jp/news/2018/08/28/national/science-health/get-ready-robot-invasion-classrooms/

Holley, P. (2015). Bill Gates on dangers of artificial intelligence: «I don't understand why some people are not concerned». Retrieved from: https://www.washingtonpost.com/news/the-switch/wp/2015/01/28/bill-gates-on-dangers-of-artificial-intelligence-dont-understand-why-some-people-are-not-concerned

Kohli, S. (2015). Bill Gates joins Elon Musk and Stephen Hawking in saying artificial intelligence is scary. *QUARTZ*. January 29, 2015. Retrieved from: https://qz.com/335768/bill-gates-joins-elon-musk-and-stephen-hawking-in-saying-artificial-intelligence-is-scary/

Lindblad, J. (1991). *Man—You, PrimordialOne and I*. Progress. Линдблад, Я. *Человек – ты, я и первозданный*.М.: Прогресс, 1991. 264 с.

Matousek, M. (2020). Elon Musk said people who don't think AI could be smarter than they are 'way dumber than they think they are. *Business insider*. July 23, 2020. Retrieved from: https://www.businessinsider.com/elon-musk-smart-people-doubt-ai-dumber-than-they-think-2020-7?utm_source=feedburner&utm_medium=feed&utm_campaign=Feed%3A+typepad%2Falleyinsider%2Fsilicon_alley_insider+%28Silicon+Alley+Insider%29

McCurry, J. (2015). Japanese bank introduces robot workers to deal with customers in branches: Mitsubishi UFJ Financial Group is employing 'Nao', a Multilingual 5.4-kg robot, who will begin work in a branch in April, *The Guardian*. Retrieved from: https://www.theguardian.com/world/2015/feb/04/japanese-bank-introduces-robot-workers-to-deal-with-customers-in-branches

Musk, Elone in Tweeter. (2020). https://twitter.com/elonmusk/status/1229546206948462597?ref_src=twsrc%5Etfw%7Ctwcamp%5Etweetembed%7Ctwterm%5E1229546206948462597%7Ctwgr%5Eshare_3&ref_url=https%3A%2F%2F

Sintschenko, V. V. (2017). *Globale Transformationen der Gegenwart*. – Band 1. *Systemischen globale Transformation: Monographie* (244 s.). Palmarium Academic Publishing.

Stern, B. (1983). Human is a… (Necessary addition to the three laws of Asimov)/Штерн, Б.Г. Человек – это… (Необходимое дополнение к трём законам Азимова). *Химия и жизнь*. № 4. С.87–92.

Suciu, P. (2015). Musk donates $10 million to keep AI from going rogue. Retrieved from: https://www.technewsworld.com/story/82239.html

Vereinte Nationen. (2015). Resolution der Generalversammlung – Transformation unserer Welt: die Agenda 2030 für nachhaltige Entwicklung 2015. Retrieved from: http://www.un.org/Depts/german/gv-70/band1/ar70001.pdf

Zinchenko, V. (2021). Sustainable development goals as an integrative basis of the global public strategy for the effectiveness of ecology, education, and science at all levels. *IOP Science: Earth and Environmental Science, 635*. Sustainable Future and Environmental Science. (2021) 012012. https://doi.org/10.1088/1755-1315/635/1/012001. Retrieved from: https://iopscience.iop.org/article/10.1088/1755-1315/635/1/012001/

Chapter 7
Challenges of University Communication Teaching in the Artificial Intelligence Age

Amaro La Rosa

Abstract The chapter starts with one panoramic view of communication as a very important activity of human beings that implies a particular representation of reality closely linked with the cultural context features and that demand an interdisciplinary explanation for their understanding, taking into account the complexity of their nature. Undoubtedly in the contemporary world, we live in a hyperconnected society, where the isolated individual is not conceived but rather establishes close ties with countless contacts. Particular challenges of communication teaching are described: First the constant changes in the world of communication, second the rapid development of knowledge in the area and its theoretical support, third the growing access to large volumes of information, and fourth the development of research methods and resources. The great threat to humanity represented by Covid-19 also affected the field of Communication: Virtuality and remote work became solutions for the crisis, which affected Communication teachers and students. Technology companies, for their part, were forced to develop more powerful platforms, innovative resources, and applications to enhance educational tasks. The adoption of IA technology in higher education teaching is analyzed showing the main advantages of their use to improve administrative and teaching procedures. Based on a preliminary analysis of Communication majors in the top ten ranked universities in Latin America, the need to introduce one Artificial Intelligence course in the study plans of Communications careers is justified by the author. Finally, a brief prospective SWOT analysis is formulated on the trends of university teaching with the support of Artificial Intelligence.

Keywords Communication teaching · Technology · Artificial intelligence

A. La Rosa (✉)
Department of Translation and Communication Science, Universidad Femenina del Sagrado Corazón, Lima, Peru
e-mail: amaro@unife.edu.pe

F. Roumate (ed.), *Artificial Intelligence in Higher Education and Scientific Research*, Bridging Human and Machine: Future Education with Intelligence,
https://doi.org/10.1007/978-981-19-8641-3_7

7.1 Introduction

Throughout history, higher education has been perfecting its teaching–learning activities by making use of the technological resources that have been invented or developed. They have been successfully applied to the various phases of the educational process. Naturally, the resources of artificial intelligence have been gradually implemented in the university environment.

The nature of the work of the communicators requires that in their professional training mastery of the technological resources of the specialty is achieved to have prepared and highly qualified human resources for the labor market. The development of applications and robots with artificial intelligence demand that the subject be included as part of the Communication curriculum.

7.2 Background

7.2.1 Human Beings and Communication

We start from the conviction that human beings are social by nature. This involves in logical terms that humankind developing a great number of communicative actions from a diverse cultural background that were analyzed along with the history of different scientific theories, disciplines, and also philosophical approaches.

Explaining communication as an everyday process of information exchange we found a close relationship with the culture. Of course, there is no universal agreement about the concept of culture and communication, but in the socialization process, the human being internalizes the particular forms of social representations of reality own of their culture, which means social perception of reality, interpretation of situations and views of situations or phenomena.

From the viewpoint of Maturana (1995), the reality is not the same for all human beings. Each individual produces differentiations by their praxis of living in the language. Translators can attest to this perspective when they try to build a text from the complexity of another, whose way of understanding reality is completely different. This is not only because of the signs used but because of the entirely different nature and practice of each language.

Of course, the complexity of social issues cannot be viewed only from the perspective of communication science. By their nature, a whole understanding of communication activity demands a holistic interdisciplinary approach.

In the history of communication media, there are many steps along the time. From our visión, the interaction between three factors could be found in this process: Communication, technology, and society. Communication means the interest to present to the community a worldview through phantasies, mythical or realistic representations of fragments of reality, Society brings the context in which the idea can be turned into reality and can be presented. Technology is the possibility to find the solution to one problem of human beings: How to send a message with the most appropriate tool?

In contemporary life, anyone is in direct contact with a limited number of aspects of reality, and this only allows a partial knowledge of the world. Nowadays mass media presents us with various perspectives of reality, developing a mediatization process between society and people. Following the objectivity of information, means the presence of an accurate version of reality. Media are vehicles through which socially shared cognitions and ways of interpreting reality are constructed. They feed the flow of public opinion creating trends. They provide objects of attention and thought, as well as explanations referring to reality. The media make the reader, listener, or viewer eyewitness to the real events that the media presents.

Without a doubt, we live now in a hyperconnected world. A great part of the people who live in urban metrópolis and also in the rural áreas have access to many technological devices that improve their possibilities to exchange information. We can use this way Mcluhan's (1964) claim that media are extensions of ourselves.

There is a need to look carefully at the role of the media concerning public opinion, which can also be conceived as a communicative process, where the community builds its appreciation of the main issues that attract its attention or are particularly interested in it. In the formation of opinion, the media plays a role that needs to be investigated. This is very important from our point of view since the free expression of public opinion is a fundamental characteristic of democratic societies.

Media are considered witnesses of humankind's history or watchdogs of society but in light of the events, they are history makers too, because in many circumstances they develop a decisive role in the implementation of political actions, public policies, or reforms that change the course of one society's life. Are very interesting to discuss the words of Castells (2007, p. 242): "The media are not the holders of power, but they constitute by and large the space where power is decided".

The great and profound technological transformations produced in the last century have developed advanced communication systems and changed human interaction. Social networks such as Facebook are channels of information exchange and the findings prove that constant appearance and number of contacts could be closely linked with credibility. The mobile phone allows rapid forms of communication patterns and has developed new forms of social mobility which make possible the expression of common ideas.

The Internet has generated changes in public opinion construction. The Internet has brought the beings of the world closer together, the world has shrunk, distances have shortened, and the most distant countries are close thanks to the Internet. With the network, the public takes an active role in communication producing users generated content. Slavoj Zizek implicitly recognizes the importance of the Internet for the current human being when he qualifies it as "the global communication network that everyone uses and that becomes the substance of their social lives" (Zizek, 2008, p. 108).

Social networking by its nature involves intercultural communication in which people of different cultures perceive and produce millions of data per day. As the result of multiple variables, the holistic understanding of these networks necessarily requires a transdisciplinary approach.

Niklas Luhmann's theory revolves around the concept of communication. By communication, he does not understand human action in Habermas's sense, not a technological phenomenon, not an exchange of information. Men cannot communicate, "only communication communicates." According to Luhmann, social systems emerge when an autopoietic communicative relationship is established. In this sense, social systems are built by communication rather than by human actions (Luhmann, 1986).

7.2.2 Communication Teaching

In university education, many teachers have not received academic training as educators and have been trained in practice. In some cases, they have had the support of a teacher with extensive experience who was their mentor and helped them to face the teaching task in its beginning and later to improve it. Others may have been true self-made men, reviewing up-to-date information and permanently attending various training activities that taught them how to run a class, what tools to use for more productive teaching, and how to properly assess their students.

The teaching of communication involves particular challenges that we will briefly describe from our point of view.

First, because the communication world is in constant change, there is a long distance between the radio broadcast that I discovered in my first experience in radio broadcasting in 1967, when the reel recorders, the vinyl discs, and the turntables were used, compared with the computers and digital devices of the contemporary digital radio. A large part of these changes is the product of the acceleration of technological development that has been taking place since the last decades of the twentieth century. Technological changes in the world of communication are part of an irreversible process that is now evident in the case of artificial intelligence.

Second, knowledge develops equally inexorably. New issues, approaches, and scientific research have grown. Let's only review the information search. When we started our teaching career we had to figure out how to find the latest information. It was an adventure looking for materials in libraries and traveling long distances in the city to find the book that was in a library at the other end of the city. Knowledge is abundant now. Now we have an information tsunami in the palm. To say it unorthodoxly: Information "search for us" with the products in which we have a particular interest. It is tailor-made knowledge, with the algorithm of this artificial intelligence age.

Third, because knowledge advances equally fast, new themes, approaches, and scientific actors emerge with a high volume of information. Only focus on data search. When we start our career our teaching career in the 70s we need to work a lot to find updated information, searching in libraries, sometimes at the other corner of our city. Now we have a tsunami of information in the palm of our hands with our smartphones. Apart from that, the algorithms are constantly feeding us with resources in which we are interested. Saying it in an unorthodox view, the system searches day after day for us with the information that interests us particularly. That is, knowledge tailored to the client.

Fourth, the research methodology has to be adapted to the new conditions. The search for data itself and the researcher's work is now favored by the enormous body of information accessible not only on web pages but also through the various instruments that the Internet offers us. By the way, this does not exempt us from a careful selection and review for which the researcher must be properly trained, since we return here to the assertion that even the most advanced technological resources for research are nothing without the explicit intervention of the competent scientist who must use it objectively and ethically to analyze the research issue.

Research is another expertise very important to motivate creativity in the students of Communication. I share with Gil (2013) the vision of research as a skill that must be developed and for that reason, skills for research must be developed gradually, from the first semesters of the career. Investigating involves appealing to sources of evidence of various kinds to arrive at the knowledge of a certain object of study that must be learned. The competencies for this task are not acquired by spontaneous generation: Worth the redundancy, one learns to investigate by investigating. This pedagogical criterion of "learning by doing" has been highlighted by UNESCO as an appropriate way to contribute to the development of a society that better understands its environment (Leicht et al., 2018). This is the basis of the formative research that is applied with success in many higher education institutions. In this regard, the 2013 World Report on Social Sciences (CICS/UNESCO, 2015, p. 4) indicates that "to continue advancing we need scientific proposals that allow us to overcome barriers between disciplines and methods."

Also, from our perspective, for university professors in charge of communication research chairs is essential to the evidence-based research approach, which involves input from the researcher's professional experience, the updated theoretical knowledge as well as the results of scientific research from various theoretical and methodological perspectives and the viewpoint of the researchers that comes from their own professional experience. Of course, this necessarily implies that research should not be taught by those who do not practice it.

The concept of the Digital Economy emerged in the 90s as a result of the impact of growing digitalization on the economy. ECLAC (CEPAL, 2013, pp. 9–10) estimates that the digital ecosystem has three basic components:

- Broadband network infrastructure.
- Industry of software, hardware, and ICT applications.
- End users (individuals, companies, and government).

In the digital economy in particular and in the information and communication society in general, the fundamental inputs are data. According to the recent Digital Economy Report 2021, "data are multidimensional. From an economic perspective, they can provide not only private value for those who collect and control the data, but also social value for the whole economy." (UNCTAD, 2021, p. 4). There is a tendency to think that in the fourth industrial revolution what is required is that a highly qualified student needs to focus appropriately on the data. From the point of view of Kusumah (2019) for the management of information in one environment in which a huge volume of data is available some skills are required:

- Access information sources.
- Select adequate information.
- Structure data.
- Analyze information.
- Formulate valid conclusions.

Akhmedov (2022) suggests the start-up of an innovative holistic strategy to ensure the adaptability of the higher education system to the constantly updated contemporary information ecosystem. To be fully prepared for the demands of professional work, communication students must develop the hard skills that allow them to use current technological resources and learn to manage new ones efficiently. Must also develop soft skills to take on teamwork, make quick decisions and innovate; always with an ethical perspective. In this sense, we share the criterion of Penprase (2018, 220): "Graduates of any 4IR higher education should be capable of advancing the material culture of our future world while creating a culture which advances technologies sustainably and ethically."

Another issue that has generated controversy is the widespread idea that communication students should be prepared to perform as multitasking professionals because this is a tendency in the labor market. In this regard, Drody et al. (2022) believe that multitasking happens in everyday life, but there is abundant evidence to suggest that we are not effective media multitaskers as a constant practice. González (2018) reports that versatility and multitasking have contributed to the low quality of the journalistic content that we can see in some media.

We believe for our part that the student must understand the various tasks of his profession. However, in their professional exercise, each one will lean toward a certain area in particular. Just as we are different human beings, each one of us has greater interest and expertise according to our abilities and preferences.

7.2.3 The Challenge of Covid-19

2020 has been a very complex and difficult year for humanity due to the Covid-19 pandemic. Sickness, death, uncertainty, abrupt changes in lifestyle, social isolation, economic impact, and fear were part of the panorama of that moment in history. However, as a disrupting situation, amid the misfortune that the pandemic brought to humanity, there was a revolution in the digital market, an acceleration in research, and an increase in collaboration in science (without which the rapid development of vaccines would not have been possible) as well as the exponential growth of training opportunities. In many cases free of fees.

The acceleration of a series of technological transformations that are essential to adjust to the new demands that this pandemic has posed in various fields. On the one hand, it has forced the accelerated digital literacy of digital migrants who wanted to stay out of technological development. Secondly, has it conditioned the acceleration of digital transformation in companies and governments? Of course, the academy itself has had to face the demands of virtual education by accessing new platforms and digitizing its administrative procedures.

Undoubtedly the coronavirus COVID-19 pandemic is the greatest challenge for contemporary society. It is a global health crisis that has a great impact on the whole everyday practices of humankind around the globe. The impact is great that many thinkers are saying that the future of life could be not the same, and clearly, human beings can talk about society before COVID-19 and society after it.

Some theoretical approaches linked with the reality of online communication in Latin America are the background for this issue because the digital divide is one of the angles. On one side professors need to reinvent their communicative and teaching skills and on the other, the students that are not homogenous in the property of technological devices need online teaching. Also, the traditional offline setting and classroom interaction are out, and it demands the searching for new forms of communication and motivational resources such as gaming to engage the students in the class.

The health emergency is forcing society to connect with new technologies and enter the digital sphere, which represents the adequate adaptation to virtual modalities and environments, which in many cases require equipment and Internet access, which are not homogeneous for all. In contexts of social inequality, the issue of virtual education will become a challenge to continue with university life.

At the moment in which this chapter is written, some problems derived from two factors can be visualized: The tensions generated by remote work and the frequent failure of students to search for information. Many resources, applications, and practical suggestions are created to manage tensions. In the case of the students, it is not worth filling students with knowledge at present, because there is access to many sources. The most important thing now is to teach them how to search for information, which demands discipline and more time learning to search and discriminate between valuable and unnecessary or false information.

7.3 AI in Communication Teaching

7.3.1 Adoption of IA Technology in Communication Teaching

The first ideas about artificial intelligence were explained 60 years ago, but now their applications in many areas of knowledge are growing exponentially in many areas of knowledge. We are not the first to use Eco (1965) terms, to assert that in the face of the evidence of the technological development that Artificial Intelligence entails, two modes of behavior could manifest people. On one side would be the apocalyptic or modern Luddites who resist its use, and continue to use obsolete resources; and on the other hand, the integrated ones, who enthusiastically adopt innovations, and even motivate others to use them. Of course, today's apocalyptics tend to be fewer and fewer and may become tomorrow's uncompromisingly integrated, because sooner or later, they will have to use the technological resources to which they potentially have access, which carries a series of advantages: They facilitate daily tasks, perfect information products and allow higher standards of competitiveness. Innovation naturally contributes to this process of inclusion, which speeds up processes and simplifies the very handling of devices and applications.

When one university thinks about technology adoption, a crucial issue is the cost–benefit ratio and the amount of investment required. It is quite true in this sense that the more recent the innovation, the more often its cost is higher. Forero (2020) states that the implementation of AI in higher education represents a high investment for any university. However, its indispensable adoption provides great benefits such as:

- Analyze student data in depth to motivate personalized and collaborative learning.
- Create algorithms that facilitate the teaching task, making more time feasible for creative work.
- Analyze trends in student performance for monitoring and individualized advice.

Seo et al. (2021) have demonstrated the complex impact of AI on learner–instructor interaction in online learning. In their research, instructors perceive more meaningful interaction, make more possible just-in-time personalized support and help instructors become more aware of students' needs.

In the specific case of Communication, teaching and improving a course in AI is an urgent need for some reasons:

- Growing adoption of AI in newsrooms
- Development of applications to analyze fake news
- Development of robots in diverse areas of Communication
- Innovation in apps for Public Relations
- The massive use of chatbots in universities
- Innovation in AI-made online publications
- Introduction of AI in design
- Introduction of AI in diverse steps of TV and cinema production.

But what academia is doing for learning and teach AI?

Focusing on Latin American Communication schools and as a preliminary diagnosis of the teaching of AI, the study plans of the first ten universities in the ranking 2022 prepared by US News College were analyzed. Reviewing the thirty-eight Communication specialties of these higher education centers, it was found that none of them there was an Artificial Intelligence course. Probably some courses may have included some class or knowledge related to AI, but an exhaustive review of the course syllabi was not carried out (Table 7.1).

Table 7.1 2022 ten best universities in Latin America

Place	University	Country	Specialties
1	Universidade de São Paulo	Brazil	4
2	Universidade Estadual de Campinas	Brazil	4
3	Pontificia Universidad Católica de Chile	Chile	3
4	Universidad Federal do Rio de Janeiro	Brazil	3
5	Universidad de Chile	Chile	2
6	Universidad de Buenos Aires	Argentina	5
7	Universidad Nacional Autónoma de México	México	5
8	Universidade Federal do Rio Grade do Sul	Brazil	4
9	Universidade Federal de Minas Gerais	Brazil	4
10	Universidade Estadual Paulista	Brazil	4

Author elaboration. *Source* USNews & World Report (2022)

For me is very important that Communication faculties include at least one course in Artificial Intelligence in their study plans. We cannot follow the preparation of students of Communications to adjust them to the needs of contemporary society. Is urgent to the future world. It requires providing them with the resources and tools to work with AI. Initially understood the algorithms and then was able to create applications for the various areas involved in the world of Communication.

Naturally, not all students will be able to be experts at a higher level of technical knowledge. But they must understand how AI can be applied in Communication. This will make it possible for them to be able to manage these resources to optimize their professional work.

Another challenge to face will be the shortage of highly qualified professionals for teaching AI in the field of Communication. This demands the training of specialists at the postgraduate level and the motivation to formulate permanent research and collaboration proposals with international institutions for teaching and research in AI.

7.3.2 Concluding Remarks: Communication Teaching in the Future

This brief intellectual adventure, in which we have tried to review the fundamental aspects related to higher education in the field of communication, concludes with a preliminary prospective vision that has been developed from the information analyzed to prepare this chapter and some outstanding ideas of the existing evidence on the subject. The idea is embodied in the SWOT analysis that we present in Fig. 7.1 which shows our prospective viewpoint of higher education teaching in

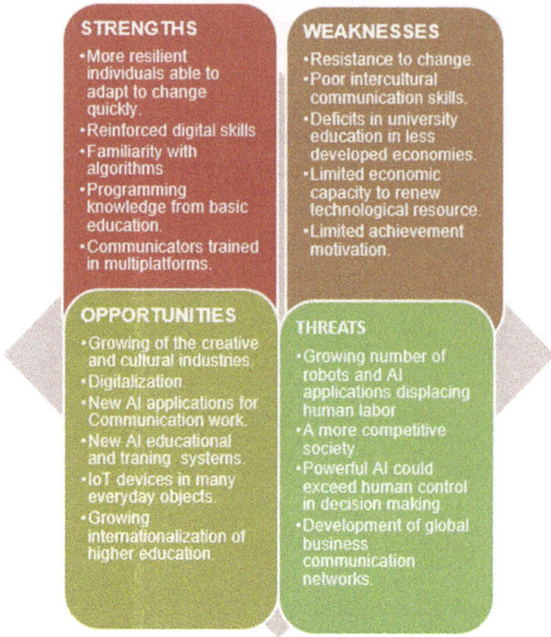

Fig. 7.1 A prospective view of communication teaching with AI support. Author elaboration

the future with AI support. Of course, we are aware that this will later require a more far-reaching prospective investigation, which we are trying to formulate.

Counting on current technological resources, it is possible to exchange exploratory investigations of students in real-time that contribute to the knowledge of their reality and others. Thus, higher education institutions would be complying with the demand made by society to "produce, among other things, socially valid scientific knowledge capable of generating creative solutions in multiple areas of social endeavor." (Royero, 2003).

The specific modalities of facing the challenges, the use we make of AI and the success we can achieve in our Communication teaching depends on us.

7.4 Conclusion

Finally, a great lesson was learned: The most advanced resources coming from Artificial Intelligence are very important for teaching and learning improvement of Communication, and surely it will have much more interesting applications to be discovered in the future. But whatever the theoretical approach from which one starts, the specific medium in which the media products are elaborated or the dimension of the communication organization in which they work, the expertise and handling of a qualified professional in Communication will be needed in the future to mix, organize and perform the resources to obtain the best final guides for the students' successful career and their full adjustment to the market requirements. Qualified higher education students with better soft skills and the best knowledge of AI will be prepared in the best conditions for their professional future. And always, as the guideline in his life, keeping solid ethical principles in his mind and his daily actions.

References

Akhmedov, B. (2022). Use of information and communication technologies in higher education: Trends in the Digital Economy. ИЖТИМОИЙ ФАНЛАРДА ИННОВАЦИЯ ОНЛАЙН ИЛМИЙ ЖУРНАЛИ (*Journal of Innovation in SocialSciences*), 71–79. Access: http://www.sciencebox.uz/index.php/jis/article/view/1365

Castells, M. (2007). Communication, power and counter-power in the network society. *International Journal of Communication, 1*, 238–266. https://ijoc.org/index.php/ijoc/article/view/46/35

CICS/UNESCO. (2015). *Informe Mundial sobre Ciencias Sociales*. UNESCO.

Comisión Economica para América Latina. (2013). *Economía digital para el cambio estructural y la igualdad*. CEPAL.

Drody, A., Ralph, B., Danckert, J. S., & Daniel. (2022). Boredom and media multitasking. *Frontiers in Psychology, 13*, 807667. https://doi.org/10.3389/fpsyg.2022.807667

Eco, U. (1965). *Apocalípticos e integrados*. Gedisa.

Forero, T. (2020). Conoce los principales impactos de la inteligencia artificial (IA) en la educación y sus posibilidades futuras. Rockcontent. March 19 2020. Access March 30, 2022. https://rockcontent.com/es/blog/inteligencia-artificial-en-la-educacion/

Gil, F. (2013). ¿Qué significa investigar?. Fondo de Cultura Económica.

González, A. (2018). Periodista multitarea, un pulpo en el que espero no convertirme. In Behar, Olga. *Periodismo universitario en el Siglo XXI* (pp. 147–162). Editorial Universidad Santiago de Cali

Kusumah, Y. (2019). The fourth industrial revolution based innovation for information and communication technology-based teaching. In *Proceedings of the Second International Conference on Social, Economy, Education, and Humanity (ICoSEEH 2019)—Sustainable Development in Developing Country for Facing Industrial Revolution 4.0* (pp. 477–482). https://doi.org/10.5220/0009439004770482

Leicht, A., Heiss, J., & Byun, W. (2018). *Issues and trends in education for sustainable development*. UNESCO.

Luhmann, N. (1986). *Ökologische Kommunikation*. Westdeutscher Verlag.

Maturana, H. (1995). *La Realidad: ¿objetiva o construida?* Editorial Anthropos.

McLuhan, M. (1964). *Understanding media*. McGraw Hill.

Penprase, B. (2018).The Fourth Industrial Revolution and Higher Education In N. Gleason (Ed.), *Higher Educatiion in the era of the fourth industrial revolution* (pp. 213–228). Palgrave Mac Millan.

Royero, J. (2003). Gestión de sistemas de investigación universitaria en América Latina. *Revista Iberoamericana De Educación, 33*(1), 1–19.

Seo, K., Tang, J., Roll, I., Fels, S., & Yoon, D. (2021). The impact of artificial intelligence on learner–instructor interaction in online learning. *International Journal of Educational Technology in Higher Education, 18*(54). https://doi.org/10.1186/s41239-021-00292-9

United Nations Conference on Trade and Development. (2021). *Digital economy report 2021 (overview)*. UNCTAD.

USNews & World Report. (2022). 2022 Best global universities in Latin America. https://www.usnews.com/education/best-global-universities/latin-america?int=top_nav_Universities_in_Latin_America. Accessed April 30, 2022.

Zizek, S. (2008). *En defensa de la intolerancia*. Ediciones Sequitur

Chapter 8
Educational Sovereignty and Artificial Intelligence Challenges: The Case of Morocco

Said Hajji

Abstract This article presents a concise and focused analysis of the most significant threats to educational sovereignty in Morocco in the age of artificial intelligence, highlighting the concept of educational sovereignty in light of the Moroccan media and the political debate on "ministries of sovereignty." The article outlines the most important initiatives and projects in Morocco to overcome the challenges threatening the educational system and educational sovereignty in the era of AI systems, which have become unavoidable tools in the learning process and classroom practices. The study focuses mainly on the effects of the use of foreign languages; the proliferation of foreign schools and transnational universities in Morocco; the impacts of the intensive use of foreign EdTech by Moroccan teachers and learners; the platforms and programs disseminated by big techs such as GAFAM (Google, Apple, Facebook, Amazon, and Microsoft); and finally, the threats posed by the absence of a national cloud computing structure for protecting digital sovereignty and safeguarding the personal data of learners and the educational system. The article attempts to argue that Morocco's plans to create a digital ecosystem capable of protecting its educational sovereignty still face many subjective and objective obstacles.

Keywords Educational sovereignty · Artificial Intelligence · Personal data · Privacy · EdTech

8.1 Methodology

This study seeks to analyze and interpret data and results in light of previous literature that has differently approached the relationship between sovereignty, education, and artificial intelligence in various ways. The study's main purpose is to highlight the aspects and particularities related to the concept of educational sovereignty. The article adopts a descriptive and analytical methodology to answer questions concerning the extent to which the country of Morocco is aware of the risks that

S. Hajji (✉)
Faculty of Law, Economic and Social Sciences Agdal, Mohammed V University, Rabat, Morocco
e-mail: hajjisaid@hotmail.com

F. Roumate (ed.), *Artificial Intelligence in Higher Education and Scientific Research*, Bridging Human and Machine: Future Education with Intelligence,
https://doi.org/10.1007/978-981-19-8641-3_8

threaten its educational sovereignty as well as the means and measures implemented to protect its digital sovereignty and the privacy of learners and teachers necessary for circumventing or reducing the most significant risks posed by the use of artificial intelligence systems. The study will serve as preliminary research to better understand a developing country's digital ecosystem model and determines its ability to protect its educational sovereignty.

8.2 Introduction

My research of previous literature on educational sovereignty and AI did not lead me to any books or scientific articles that investigated the question of educational sovereignty in the era of AI with focus; neither studies carried out in Morocco nor those conducted abroad proved to be useful, except for the report by Levet (2019) on the situation in France concerning EdTech in particular. However, the three following reviews have been very beneficial to me concerning the central subject they deal with.

The first book is *Educational Sovereignty and Transnational Exchanges in Post-Secondary Indonesian Education* by Abbott (2017). The importance of this book for my research lies in its ability to distinguish between the general concept of sovereignty, which is a characteristic of the state, and the specific meaning of educational sovereignty. Besides the precise details that the book provides on the characteristics and features of educational sovereignty, the author offers a clear view of the implications of educational exchange for educational sovereignty in Indonesia; the role of transnational education in perpetuating the dependency; and the role of state and non-state actors in addressing the threat to the sovereignty of education by importing foreign educational experiences. The book's conclusions can be applied to the context of Morocco, which has lately allowed foreign capital and too many schools and international university campuses to enter the national market and compete with the Moroccan educational system.

The second book is An Introduction to Artificial Intelligence in Education by Shengquan and Yu (2021). Even though the book does not directly address the implications of AI for educational sovereignty, it introduces readers to the latest findings on the scope of AI in education. It also showcases several AI systems and products used for education. The book discusses how AI can deliver breakthrough technology in critical aspects of education, providing benefits to both learners and content, learning and teaching strategies, tools, and the environment, as well as what breakthroughs and advances are in the future of AI systems.

The third work concerns a report entitled *Preserving Our Educational Sovereignty: Supporting French EdTech*, elaborated by Levet (2019) who is a pioneer of the Internet in France, with more than 20 years of professional experience in the new technologies sector. Through this study, she urged French and European officials to initiate a deep and fast transformation of education to incorporate better training in twenty-first century skills by investing in companies that make innovations in the education sector, from school to the professional sector, and continuing training. To preserve educational sovereignty, Levet calls for deploying an ambitious digital education policy based on a robust French digital sector, capable of beating the GAFAM in terms of quality, ethics, and values, by adopting three priorities for action: build a sustainable base, facilitate public purchasing by promoting market decentralization, and make education a state investment priority. Regardless of the methodology by which this work was carried out, it contains very useful information resulting from the thorough experience of fieldwork in digital technology and investment in educational technology. Moreover, the report describes part of the Moroccan reality, addressing, above all, common concerns about the attack on digital sovereignty and its impact on the culture, education, and privacy of generations of learners and teachers.

In this article, we will focus on the efforts made by Moroccan authorities to protect the nation's educational sovereignty by addressing the main hypothesis associated with the central research question of the challenges and risks posed by artificial intelligence systems to educational sovereignty in Morocco. We will first try to explain the concept of educational sovereignty and some of the impacts of AI on education by describing the most important risks AI systems pose to the entire educational process. Then, we will focus on the case of Morocco to analyze five fundamental threats posed by artificial intelligence systems to educational sovereignty, namely the level of awareness of elites in Morocco of the importance of educational sovereignty; educational sovereignty in Morocco's legislative and regulatory texts; foreign languages and transnational universities; EdTech; and finally, digital ecosystem and cloud computing.

(a) ***State Sovereignty and Educational Sovereignty***

The concept of sovereignty has been marked, since it first appeared, by many moments of crisis and contests through which its meaning has been redefined many times. Morocco is, in fact, one of the rare countries in the Global South that attached great importance to the concept of sovereignty very early. Moroccan political discourse on the concept of "ministries of sovereignty" (Zemni & Koenraad, 2006) in successive governments since independence gave rise to the first premises of an immature debate on the issue of educational sovereignty that has not yet evolved into a real debate between academics and policymakers and has not been on the agenda of Moroccan political parties, despite the legitimate questions raised at the time by some observers as to why the monarchs of Morocco, after Independence, did not make a clear decision to join the portfolio of the Ministry of Education to the list of the rest of the ministries they considered sovereign. And since the first decade of the twenty-first century, and in light of globalization, digitization, and the spread of artificial intelligence systems and social networking sites, the concepts of digital transformation, digital sovereignty, cybersecurity, digital security, and technological sovereignty have become more attractive to specialists, while educational sovereignty is gradually gaining more interest in the circles of trade unionists, academics, teachers, and politicians.

Sovereignty is a political concept that derives from the Latin term "superanus," via the French "souveraineté." It refers to a supreme type of power that admits nothing above itself. At first glance, the definition of sovereignty may appear simple, but history shows that many attempts have been made to define and redefine the term. "The concept of sovereignty was formulated by sixteenth and seventeenth century political theorists, Jean Bodin and Thomas Hobbes, and fully developed as popular sovereignty distinct from the government, by Jean-Jacques Rousseau" (Achilleos & Balasopoulos, 2021, pp. 17–18). Over time, it has become increasingly associated with democracy, the people's will, and the rule of law. Today, sovereignty always primarily means a state's independence vis-à-vis other states. However, the concept in the era of globalization, digital transformation, and AI is no longer only attached to the whole state and has become linked to sectors within the same state. Consequently, the unique sovereignty of the state evolved into several sovereignties but under the same authority, in contrast with Bodin's principle of "indivisibility of sovereignty and the consequent, only possible dichotomous distinction between sovereign/non-sovereign states," whereby "it is unclear whether and how to determine that a state is not sovereign" (Pusterla, 2018, p. 119). Also, "this reversal of the classic vision of sovereignty—conceived until now only on the scale of a human community—undoubtedly constitutes a paradigm shift. This is a direct consequence of the process of 'reontologizing' notions induced by digital technology" (Ganascia et al., 2018, p. 36). It should be noted here that sovereignty, when associated with other concepts like food, health, technology, education, and security, takes other meanings, such as the ability to control, autonomy, independence, and self-sufficiency. By transposing the question of sovereignty to education, the main aim that constitutes our debate here is to know not only who has decision-making power over education and AI systems and technologies, their policies and plans, their development and uses, their access and distribution, and their offers and consumption but also why and how to protect educational sovereignty in the era of AI. Before that, let us examine what exactly educational sovereignty means.

There is no precise and clear definition of educational sovereignty, but the term refers to the ability to control one's educational destiny. Education not only enables transmitting from one generation to another the ideas and principles for the development of the personality and social integration of the individual, but it is also a powerful tool for reducing poverty and inequality, improving health and social well-being, enhancing identity, and achieving economic growth.

According to Abbott, educational sovereignty "involves both the maintenance and development of local cultural values through education and state authority to control the movement of people, educational materials, and institutions within and across borders" and also "refers to a state's refusal to accept foreign intervention in education unless it has sought and agreed to that intervention" (2018, pp. 17–18). This definition is consistent with the meaning of sovereignty provided in Chapter I of the United Nations Charter (UN, n.d.), which links sovereignty to two fundamental principles: the equality of all states and non-interference with the internal affairs of another nation.

Many critics believe that educational sovereignty and public education in particular are targets of neoliberals and globalists who propagate an offensive discourse against the public school system and underestimate its capacity to progress and adapt to the digital and AI age (Puiggrós, 2010). On the other hand, defenders of the public school system believe that the instrumentalization of international assessment programs of systems and students such as the Program for International Student Assessment (PISA) has the objective of penetrating the educational systems of many countries by publishing international classifications based on inaccurate criteria, aimed at encouraging public schools and universities to adhere to international programs and objectives and to push them to acquire educational technologies manufactured by big EdTech companies. For them, the globalization of education contributes to the destruction of independent educational systems and the replacement of the functions of traditional educational systems by digital systems, which constitutes a flagrant attack on educational sovereignty and the sovereignty of the state in general.

As different as the visions and positions on the issue of educational sovereignty may be, it remains "closely linked to state sovereignty for several reasons" (Abbott, 2017, p. 41). Morrow and Torres identify six criteria and features for measuring the maintenance of the presence of education sovereignty, focusing primarily on the "autonomy to regulate national education and control over national educational law without intervention from foreign authorities; the authority and control over educational materials and programs across borders and within the state's territory; and the ability to refuse intervention in education from outside the state" (Abbott, 2017, p. 42).

Given the importance of the aforementioned standards, we will use them as benchmarks to examine to what extent they correspond to the reality of the educational system as well as to what extent Morocco has succeeded in preserving its educational sovereignty in the face of the dangers caused by the massive use of artificial intelligence systems.

(b) **AI risks to Education**

The integration of technology in schools has long been a controversial topic, fuelling debates about the impact of technology on both the teaching and learning process. Currently, with the emergence of one of the most revolutionary technologies in history, AI, the debate is hotter than ever before. Moreover, policymakers and educators have entered uncharted territory that raises fundamental questions on how the future of learning will interact with AI (UNESCO, 2021). So, what is AI?

European Commission's definition of AI seems to have presented an updated and appropriate definition: "AI refers to systems designed by humans that, given a complex goal, perceive their environment, interpret the collected structured or unstructured data, reason on the knowledge derived from this data, and decide the best action(s) to take (according to pre-defined parameters) to achieve the given goal" (European Commission, 2018).

As already pointed out at the beginning of the article, this research only deals with the risks of AI on educational sovereignty. Admittedly, it is impossible to mention all the risks with the knowledge that the notion of sovereignty, including its other very specific meanings, has a constitutional and legal character. Among the major risks that could jeopardize the entire education system is, above all, the security of digital data, or what is commonly called digital sovereignty. Experts focusing on cybercrime and AI systems identify at least three major risks linked globally to issues of traceability, credibility, and transparency. Traceability or untraceability in the application of AI represents both a violation of personal privacy and, at the same time, points to an inability to identify the identity of the criminal and the itinerary of the crime (Larsson & Heintz, 2020). Inserting biased programs and fraudulent algorithms into the decision-making process or somewhere in the educational operation is also one of the most destructive risks to the credibility of the outcomes if data sources are not sufficiently protected from violations (Cukurova et al., 2019), as most designers and producers of AI systems impose strict secrecy on the algorithms they use and the data sources they analyze, like "black boxes" whose secrets can never be revealed. The lack of transparency makes it very difficult for any judicial follow-up and accountability and, in some cases, impossible (Pant et al., 2015).

These risks may be part of the working system when it comes to the banking sector, e-commerce, tourism, or any other sector, but the inability to circumvent dangers threatening a strategic sector such as education can lead to disastrous consequences, jeopardizing the educational sovereignty of a country and the future of generations of learners. Naturally, educators are called upon to develop their working methods and to choose the best pathways to optimize learning. However, decision-makers who are responsible for protecting public security are also called upon to inspect the impact of the use of AI systems on the sovereignty of the state and the security of citizens.

To align itself with the Fourth Industrial Revolution and reap the benefits of the appropriate use of AI systems as well as avoid the impacts and implications of the misuse of AI, several strategic initiatives have been launched to accelerate the digital transformation in Morocco and to register the country in a "Digital Nation approach". (Transition Numérique et de la Réforme de l'Administration, 2021). Since 2019, Morocco has also been involved in the program launched by the OECD (OECD, n.d.), whose AI principles encourage innovative and reliable use of AI that respects human rights and democratic values (OECD AI Policy Observatory Portal, n.d.). The "New Maroc digital 2020 strategy" (UNESCO, 2021) and the creation of the "Digital Development Agency" are responsible for implementing the State's digital development strategy as well as promoting digital tools and developing their use among the administration, businesses, and citizens to reflect the government's commitment. On the other hand, the Interactive Digital Center in Morocco (IDC Morocco), inaugurated on February 11, 2020, aims to establish, under the format of a public–private partnership, an innovative academy for the training and deployment of trades in the economy of digital technology, in particular, virtual and augmented reality (VAR) technologies (EON Reality, 2022). IDC Morocco develops knowledge transfer solutions in the field of virtual reality (VR) and augmented reality (AR) technologies for various academic and professional training programs to contribute to the development of skills necessary for Industry 4.0 and the expansion of the digital economy in both the national and regional level (Centre Interactif Digital-Benguerir (IDC) & Agence de Développement du Digital, n.d.).

The effort made thus far by Morocco to progress in the digital transformation project does not, by any means, mean that it has succeeded in ensuring or preserving its digital sovereignty. Moroccan digital sovereignty needs long-term work in addition to the mobilization of colossal financial resources. In this regard, several think tanks created by several experts, academics, and researchers specializing in the digital field and dedicated to various issues related to the kingdom's digital transformation explain that achieving digital sovereignty means Morocco's technological autonomy.

Whether it is to strengthen technological sovereignty, data sovereignty, digital sovereignty, or artificial intelligence systems expertise, altogether, they contribute to reinforcing educational sovereignty and making it resistant to any penetration or attempt of subversion. However, first and foremost, Morocco's educational system requires more basic reforms to preserve its educational sovereignty (OECD, 2018). Let's now look at how AI endangers Moroccan educational sovereignty.

8.3 Discussion

Artificial intelligence (AI) and robotics are breakthrough technologies that deeply transform education and impact educational sovereignty. Concerning this, five ideas ought to be discussed in the case of Morocco:

1. **Educational Sovereignty and AI in the Main Official Moroccan Educational Legislative and Regulatory Texts**

The examination of the main legislative and regulatory texts that govern and frame the education sector in Morocco reflects a total absence of a concept of educational sovereignty, not only as an objective among other objectives of educational reform but also as a strategy aimed at immunizing education against all possible threats. In the same context, the aforementioned texts make no reference to AI systems as modern tools of education, regarding neither their importance nor their contribution to educational development. Education is associated with technology only through general and vague texts that generally mention the need to develop education based on digital and modern technological means.

The Framework Law No. 51.17 on the education, training, and scientific research system ("Cent-neuvièmeAnnée," n.d.) and particularly the "Strategic Vision of Reform, 2015–2030," which is drawn up by The Higher Council for Education, Training, and Scientific Research—an independent advisory body established by Article 168 of the Constitution responsible for issuing its opinion on all public policies and questions of national interest concerning education, training, and scientific research, which "seeks to establish a new school set on three major pillars: equity and equality of opportunities; education quality for all; and the promotion of individuals and society" (CSEFRS, n.d.), and "submitting education to quality requirements is one of the Strategic Vision" (Bourqia, 2018). It is easy to notice that the term "quality" is used as a keyword in all the guidance reports, but it has not been explained in detail. On the other hand, there are multiple allusions in the report to educational technology, digital libraries, digital resources, networks, communication systems, distance education, and the necessity of integrating technology and digital tools into the educational process, as explained in the following paragraph: "The integration of educational technologies aims to qualify the learner to access the knowledge society, to master the strategies of distance education, and to build personal projects at the level of research and innovation; to rationalize educational governance by relying on integrated information systems" (Le Conseil supérieur de l'Education de la Formation et de la Recherche Scientifique, n.d.). And unlike the previous two reports, the "New Development Model Report" reflects a positive shift in the Moroccan state's understanding of the concept of national sovereignty (La Commission Spéciale sur le Modèle de Développement, 2018). The word "sovereignty" appeared 16 times in the report, in different contexts, referring to territorial sovereignty, digital sovereignty, energy sovereignty, food sovereignty, and health sovereignty, while educational sovereignty was never mentioned in the report. Another positive observation is that the report discusses AI twice, while the term "education" is mentioned more than 50 times.

2. **AI, Language, and Educational Sovereignty**

Certainly, the national language is also a symbol of sovereignty. Since its independence, Morocco has chosen French and English as the two foreign languages, besides Arabic, which is the official national language, while the Amazigh language is rarely used in administration.

After many years of Arabisation, and instead of continuing to strengthen the position of the mother tongue as the main language in teaching, Morocco opened up to foreign languages. Unlike all successful and leading educational systems in the world, the Moroccan government recently decided to return to teaching scientific materials in French and English in the International Baccalaureate curriculum ("Framework Note", 2014), despite the great controversy that accompanied this decision defenders for the protection of the Arabic language. Language is not only a means of communication but also a vector of values, culture, identity, and sovereignty: "Sovereignty is key to the protection of every aspect of Indigenous ways of life, including cultural integrity. The ongoing loss of language and culture threatens the core principle of tribal sovereignty" (Rudiger, 2020). And as long as Morocco officially has decided to teach science and technology materials in a language other than the mother tongue, the threats to linguistic sovereignty, which is an essential element of educational sovereignty, increase proportionally with the number of learners and teachers dependent on foreign educational systems and projects, carried out by transnational universities[1], mission schools, and powerful educational technology firms. Morocco, for reference, is among the largest hosts of university branch campuses and mission schools in Africa, in addition to having a large national university, private schools and universities ("List", 2013), and large educational and research not-for-profit centers. The English language, for its part, monopolizes a large part of the innovations of

AI systems, tightens the noose even more on educational sovereignty, and makes it the prey of foreign interference as the globally dominant language of teaching and learning or as the language most used by EdTech, social networks and digital platforms, despite the great opportunities offered by globalization and the technological revolution of AI systems across all fields, including electronic translation and high-efficiency text translation.

3. **EdTech: A Double-Edged Sword for Educational Sovereignty**

The COVID-19 pandemic has demonstrated more than ever before that school is no longer the only source and place of learning. The latest technological advances, particularly innovative platforms and AI systems, have imposed themselves as alternatives to conventional educational methods. Furthermore, disruptive education is now one of the watchwords of the twenty-first century that seeks to guarantee learners' access to digital domains by customizing learning, reinforcing digital skills among learners, and integrating AI throughout the educational process. EdTech, a contraction of "educational technology", whose "approaches have evolved from early uses of audiovisual aids to individual and networked computers, and now has evolved to include various mobile and smart technologies, as well as virtual and augmented realities, avatar-based immersive environments, cloud computing, and wearable and location-aware devices" (Huang et al., 2019), is an ecosystem of different actors: public and private institutions, companies, users, and in particular startups, participating in the development and integration of technological components in education or training processes, on different scales and in different areas, which currently form the ideal means to implement disruptive education goals.

Despite all the benefits that the education sector can reap from what startups and big techs like GAFAM provide, the negative effects of educational technology on the teaching and learning process cannot be overlooked. The excessive reliance on technology and ready-made programs dehumanizes the teaching and limits learners' opportunities to develop writing, analytical, and critical-thinking skills. It also exacerbates several problems related to the difficulty of students' integration into society. On the other hand, the inability of a large number of students to access the Internet deepens the gap between students, especially in developing countries.

GAFAM, BATX (Baidu, Alibaba, Tencent, and Xiaomi.), and NATUs (Netflix, Airbnb, Tesla, and Uber), (Gilibert, 2021) are criticized not only for their anti-competitive practices and hegemony over AI among other digital domains that threaten state sovereignty but also, along with EdTech, for their attempts to replace traditional educational models and their actors with new concepts and models likely to achieve key objectives, namely the digitization, personalization, and automation of education, and above all, globalization, which allows the blurring of borders and cultural and educational particularities between people with the major and undeclared goal of commodifying education.

In Morocco, the intensive and extensive use of digital technology in learning and teaching practices in recent years is an indisputable fact. The COVID-19 crisis has accelerated tremendous access to educational innovations and technological tools and brought out new uses and concepts such as online courses via Zoom, Google

Meet, and Skype, educational platforms such as Moodle, Canvas, Google Classroom, Additi, Flipgrid, and Genially, and multi-platform mobile applications that enable encrypted instant messaging like WhatsApp, Messenger, Instagram, etc. Distance education, the online monitoring of learners (MapNews, n.d.), and the evaluation of distance training from primary to university level have turned the lives of learners and professionals upside down.

Aware of these technological transformations and challenges and their consequences for education, the government and the Ministry of National Education have undertaken, within their means, several initiatives and partnerships to support these transformations by trying to provide a favorable ecosystem of educational technologies conducive to the implementation of innovative educational concepts adapted to local realities and educational needs. Perhaps the most important of these initiatives is the creation at the Mohamed VI Polytechnic University in Bengrir (University Mohammed VI Polytechnic, n.d.) of a center of excellence in AI called The Moroccan International Center for AI (The Moroccan International Center for Artificial Intelligence, n.d.), which "aims to foster the emergence of Moroccan expertise in AI and Data Sciences," and "it is both an articulating and consolidating tool of various actions related to the field of AI, with the ambition of making Morocco a regional AI hub impacting its ecosystem on strategic, educational, and industrial levels and a lever to anticipate and accompany the evolutions and transformations related to AI and Data Sciences" (The Moroccan International Center for Artificial Intelligence, n.d.). The second most important initiative involves encouraging the creation of Moroccan EdTech (Mohamed, 2018), in partnership with private and public sector players, urging active telecommunications companies to support schools (Challenge, 2022), linking them to the Internet, and encouraging teachers' initiatives to produce digital resources and educational applications to create websites dedicated to education and training (Maroc. ma, 2021). Of course, the government and all supervisory authorities related to education have not raised the threshold of their ambitions to a level that even the European Union countries could not even implement, which for years have been calling for a "European Google" and creating strong European EdTech companies able to compete with those of the USA, China, and India.

Morocco believes that these initiatives, as modest as they are, can contribute to progressively improving the Moroccan digital ecosystem and give a boost to Moroccan startups in EdTech[2] by supporting them in producing applications adapted to local needs and international security standards, to reduce the significant risks to educational sovereignty and data security posed by the applications of GAFAM companies widely used by Moroccan students and teachers.

4. The need for a Moroccan "sovereign computing Cloud" to protect national educational data

When discussing educational sovereignty in the age of AI, we automatically think of the ability to protect the personal data of learners and teachers as well as the data of the rest of the education sector's supervisory authorities. This ability refers to the government's efforts to prevent learners' and teachers' data from falling into the wrong hands by implementing strict measures that limit any form of illicit transfer of personal data across borders. This raises questions about who hosts this data, who controls its storage, and who has the authority to process and use it. It is known that there is a close relationship between big data and AI, as the latter needs a huge amount of data to learn and improve decision-making processes. The collection of data by automation and AI systems is furthermore necessary to develop AI and machine learning algorithms to understand the trends of students and better predict their tendencies. This explains the behavior of GAFAM and EdTech companies that record and store all data traces that students and teachers might leave when using any kind of connected device: computers, tablets, smartphones, search browsers, or social media platforms. Moreover, all secrets and personal data such as credit card codes, traces of places visited using GPS, list of favorite websites, hobbies, and personal accounts on social networks, as well as all the requests and exchanges on the web, including chats, video conferencing, personal photos, food and clothing preferences, and even worse all the research and discussions made on the net that can reveal religious, political, and cultural beliefs and convictions and even the psychological state of the users, are stored and processed. In other words, "the machines interacting with students will know about students' strengths and qualities, foibles and personality traits, hidden weaknesses and vulnerabilities. They will know what topics or choice of words will resonate with them and persuade them to agree to do or say something they might not otherwise choose" (Seldon & Abidoye, 2020). With this huge and accurate data, GAFAMs and EdTech companies can know everything about the lives of learners and their teachers, track their biographies since childhood, and even draw accurate profiles (The Guardian, 2017), like complete ID cards with the most important private data about them. This is only a small part of the dark side of educational technology (The Edvocate, 2018), and some studies and intelligence reports have revealed its potential risks.

Of course, the risks regarding collecting private and personal data from students and teachers cause concern across the world, not only in Morocco, despite some attempts to regulate this use. In November 2021, the member states of UNESCO at the General Conference adopted the first-ever global standard on the ethics of artificial intelligence. The agreement defines the common values and principles that will guide the construction of the necessary legal infrastructure to ensure the healthy development of AI (Recommendation on the Ethics of Artificial Intelligence) (UNESCO, n.d.). Further, the AI Act (2021), which is a proposed European law on artificial intelligence (AI), is the first law on AI by a major regulator anywhere, in addition to the General Data Protection Regulation (GDPR) enacted by the European Union to regulate the processing of personal data in the European Union (GDPR, 2019). However, in the absence of an autonomous digital ecosystem and an EdTech that does not outsource to international Chinese and American companies, digital sovereignty remains compromised and at the mercy of private companies. "The unlimited storage size that the cloud offers enables unprecedented computing power and storage" (Yu, 2022), so the problem of data storage or the so-called sovereign cloud (Tech Monitor, 2019) is capable of providing security, access, and control to data without the risk of alteration, deletion, copying, or disclosure of its content to unauthorized third parties, which is of great importance and also a key factor in achieving digital and educational sovereignty. This huge amount of information could constitute a database for the future that could have serious implications for the security and sovereignty of the state, especially when we remember the accusations against GAFAM companies in the scandals of leaking citizens' data during the US elections (Financial Times, 2020) and the Brexit referendum.

Data hosting is an integral part of information protection and educational as well as digital sovereignty. To implement the national digital transformation strategy of the Moroccan ecosystem and to acquire a Moroccan cloud, OCP S.A. (OCP GROUP, n.d.) and UM6P (University Mohammed VI Polytechnic, n.d.) joined forces to create the Maroc DataCenter, a certified Tier III and Tier IV by the Uptime Institute, and also integrated the most powerful supercomputer in Africa named the African Supercomputing Center in 2017, placing Morocco in the world's Top 100 smart centers.

8.4 Conclusions

(a) Concerning the debate in Morocco about the ministries of sovereignty, there seems to be a misunderstanding of sovereignty that confuses monarchic sovereignty, state sovereignty, and people's sovereignty. Perhaps the best description of the so-called ministries of sovereignty in Morocco is the "reserved domain" (of the King) (Bendourou, 2012), which "refers to a legal fiction that the President of the Republic has exclusive and undivided powers in matters of foreign policy or defense." However, no article of the Constitution expressly confers such powers on him "whether it is a matter of sovereignty" (Etudier, n.d.) or the "reserved domain" of the King (Azbeg, 2015), the Ministry of Education in Morocco has never enjoyed the same status as the Ministries of the Interior, Foreign Affairs, or Islamic Affairs, just as it has never been classified as a ministry of sovereignty, and it has often been run intermittently by political ministers or by technocrats depending on the political conjuncture. It should be emphasized here that the protection of educational sovereignty stems primarily from the recognition that education is a strategic sector and an essential component of national sovereignty.

(b) The Moroccan education sector's budget for the year 2022 amounts to 62.451 billion dirhams ("Loi de Finances", n.d.), an increase of 6% (3.591 billion dirhams) compared to 2021. Paradoxically, Morocco still has low international rankings on education and training (The Program for International Student Assessment—PISA—placed Morocco 75th out of 79 in 2019) (Education GPS, 2019). While China, the USA, and many developing countries allocate huge budgets to win the AI race, the Moroccan government has not allocated any specific investment in its recent financial laws to develop AI systems or create and finance educational technology startups. Except for some initiatives taken by some public sectors, it seems that the government does not have the interest to allocate public investments for artificial intelligence projects through specific sections in the state budget and sectoral budgets to support talented projects in the field of artificial intelligence and projects for teachers and learners, especially in innovative education and educational technology, which meet the needs of the Moroccan school system and reduce dependency on foreign companies. As for private investments in the field, they are still not competitive, either because they do not have enough funds or because they are affiliated with foreign companies investing in AI.

(c) Favoring foreign languages (French and English) to the detriment of the mother tongue (Arabic) in the teaching of scientific and technical materials; the insufficient control of flows from foreign schools and supranational universities; and the non-supervision of programs provided by private schools and supranational universities are factors that undermine linguistic sovereignty (McCarthy, 2013), aggravate educational vassalage, and multiply the risks that threaten educational sovereignty in Morocco.

(d) Despite the efforts made by Morocco, especially after the establishment of a huge data center (Maroc DataCenter), which gives consultations to the public sector as well as to private companies, stores data securely and sustainably, and hosts and provides advanced cloud services (Maroc DataCenter, n.d.), Morocco still has a long way to go to develop its digital infrastructure and strengthen its digital ecosystem. It should also pay more attention to developing and updating legislation and data protection laws, training engineers in the field, attracting talented experts, and benefiting from successful international experience in the management of artificial intelligence systems in all fields, especially education.

(e) Preserving sovereignty is ultimately a political decision. Also, educational sovereignty cannot be separated from political sovereignty as it is not possible to achieve educational sovereignty in the age of artificial intelligence without also achieving technological sovereignty, digital sovereignty, data sovereignty, and linguistic sovereignty. All these factors are harmonious and merged with the sovereignty of the state. There is no doubt that it is impossible in the era of globalization and the widespread use of applications, digital platforms, and artificial intelligence systems in all aspects of life to achieve educational sovereignty without gaps in an interdependent and constantly changing world.

Whatever the variation in the degree of effects of the above-mentioned factors on educational sovereignty, remissness in protecting and consolidating educational sovereignty certainly has a very high cost on the economy, the cultural and civilizational identity of nations, as well as the sovereignty of the state in general. The cost will be high as well as the digital divide increases even more in a rapidly changing environment dominated by digital technology and artificial intelligence systems.

References

Abbott, A. (2017). *Educational sovereignty and transnational exchanges in post-secondary Indonesian education.* Springer International Publishing.

Achilleos, S., & Balasopoulos, A. (2021). *Reading texts on sovereignty: Textual moments in the history of political thought*. Bloomsbury Academic.

Azbeg, H. S. (2015). *Processus de démocratisation et Monarchie Constitutionnelle au Maroc* [thesis].

Bendourou, O. (2012). La consécration de la monarchie gouvernante. *L'Année Du Maghreb, VIII*, 391–404.https://doi.org/10.4000/anneemaghreb.1539

Bourqia, R. (2018, April 1). *Repenser et refonder l'école au Maroc: La vision stratégique 2015–2030*. Revue internationale d'éducation de Sèvres. http://journals.openedition.org/ries/4551

Centre Interactif Digital-Benguerir (IDC) & Agence de Développement du Digital. (n.d.). *Centre Interactif digital-benguerir (IDC), Consistance/Périmètre du projet (IDC).* https://www.add.gov.ma/centre-interactif-digital-benguerir-idc

Challenge. (2022, May 23). *Enseignement numérique. Inwi et le ministère de l'Éducation nationale signent UN partenariat.* https://www.challenge.ma/enseignement-numerique-inwi-et-le-ministere-de-leducation-nationale-signent-un-partenariat-232767/

CSEFRS. (n.d.). *Abstract—csefrs.ma.* https://www.csefrs.ma/wp-content/uploads/2015/05/Re%CC%81sume%CC%81-vision-Anglais.pdf

Cukurova, M., Luckin, R., & Kent, C. (2019). Impact of an artificial intelligence research frame on the perceived credibility of educational research evidence. *International Journal of Artificial Intelligence in Education, 30,* 205–235. https://doi.org/10.1007/s40593-019-00188-w

Education GPS. (2019). *Morocco—student performance (Pisa 2018).* https://gpseducation.oecd.org/CountryProfile?primaryCountry=MAR&treshold=5&topic=PI

EON Reality. (2022, May 9). IDC Morocco, IDC & VR Innovation Academy. Retrieved April 17, 2022, from https://eonreality.com/locations/ben-guerir-ma/

Etudier. (n.d.). *Le Domaine Réservé.* https://www.etudier.com/dissertations/Le-Domaine-R%C3%A9serv%C3%A9/176303.html

European Commission. (2018). *A definition of (AI): Main capabilities and scientific disciplines. Definition developed for the deliverables of the High-Level Expert Group on AI.* https://ec.europa.eu/futurium/en/system/files/ged/ai_hleg_definition_of_ai_18_december_1.pdf

Financial Times. (2020, October 20). *US election: Facebook's political balancing act.* https://www.ft.com/content/ebbf9be3-307b-4fdd-a582-069099e3096c

Framework Note for the International Baccalaureate Courses Correspondence No. 14-133-201. Note in Arabic. Forums d'orientations. (2014, October 1). https://www.tawjihnet.net/vb/threads/15449/

Ganascia, J.-G., Germain, E., & Kirchner, C. (2018). *La souveraineté à l'ère du Numérique rester maîtres de Nos Choix et de nos valeurs*, p. 36. https://www.allistene.fr/files/2019/05/55708_AvisSouverainete-CERNA-2018.pdf

GDPR. (2019, February 22). *A guide to GDPR data privacy requirements.* https://gdpr.eu/data-privacy/

Gilibert, A. (2021, October 18). *Qui sont ces "GAFAM", "Natu", "BATX" Dont tout le monde parle?* ISLEAN. https://islean-consulting.fr/fr/transformation-digitale/gafam-natu-batx-numerique/

Huang, R., Spector, J., & Yang, J. (2019). *Educational technology: A primer for the 21st century.* Springer.

La Commission Spéciale sur le Modèle de Développement. (2018). *The new development model—CSMD.* https://www.csmd.ma/documents/CSMD_Report_EN.pdf

Larsson, S., & Heintz, F. (2020, May 5). Transparency in artificial intelligence. *Internet Policy Review, 9*(2). https://policyreview.info/concepts/transparency-artificial-intelligence

Le conseil supérieur de l'Education de la Formation et de la Recherche scientifique. (n.d.). Vision stratégique de la réforme 2015–2030. https://www.csefrs.ma/wp-content/uploads/2017/09/Vision_VF_Fr.pdf

Levet, M.-C. (2019). *Préserver notre souveraineté éducative : Soutenir l'EdTech.* Digital New Deal. https://www.thedigitalnewdeal.org/wp-content/uploads/Souverainete-educative_DigitalNewDealFoundation.pdf

List of private higher education establishments authorized by the M.E.S.F.C.R.S. (2013). Retrieved April 16, 2022, from https://web.archive.org/web/20131005050439, http://www.enssup.gov.ma/doc_site/documents/Enseignement_superieur/prive/Liste_etab_autorises.pdf

Loi de Finances du Maroc au titre de l'année 2022. (n.d.). https://www.finances.gov.ma/Publication/db/2022/BO_7049-bis_Fr.pdf

Maroc.ma. (2021, January 14). *Intelligence Artificielle (programme Al Khawarizmi): 45 projets profitent d'un appui de 50 MDH*. https://www.maroc.ma/fr/actualites/intelligence-artificielle-programme-al-khawarizmi-45-projets-profitent-dun-appui-de-50

Maroc Datacenter. (n.d.). *Moroccan Datacenter presentation. Le meilleur de l'hébergement au Maroc.* https://www.marocdatacenter.ma/about-mdt.php

McCarty, T. L. (2013). 7. Education policy, citizenship, and linguistic sovereignty in Native America. In *Language Policies and (Dis)Citizenship* (pp. 116–142). Multilingual Matters.https://doi.org/10.21832/9781783090204-008

Ministre de la Transition Numérique et de la Réforme de l'Administration. (2021, December 21). *Cérémonie d'ouverture de la conférence annuelle moroccoai* [Video]. YouTube. https://www.youtube.com/watch?v=0cdIxX1UCVk&t=251s

Mohamed, A. (2018, December 3). *A quand la révolution edtech au Maroc: Les dix facteurs de blocage.* LinkedIn. Retrieved May 14, 2022, from https://fr.linkedin.com/pulse/quand-la-r%C3%A9volution-edtech-au-maroc-les-dix-facteurs-de-mohamed

OECD. (2018). *Digital Government Review of Morocco: Laying the foundations for the digital transformation of the public sector in Morocco: Read online.* OECD. https://read.oecd-ilibrary.org/governance/digital-government-review-of-morocco_9789264298729-en#page5

OECD AI Policy Observatory Portal. (n.d.). https://oecd.ai/fr/dashboards/countries/Morocco

Office Chérifien des Phosphates (Groupe). OCPGROUP. (n.d.). Retrieved May 16, 2022, from https://www.ocpgroup.ma/

Pant. R. R., Prakash, G., & Farooquie, J. A. (2015). A framework for traceability and transparency in the dairy supply chain networks. *Procedia—Social and Behavioral Sciences, 189*, 385–394. https://www.sciencedirect.com/science/article/pii/S1877042815020285/pdf?md5=228e13feb1b241147a9f966f5ed3976b&pid=1-s2.0-S1877042815020285-main.pdf

Puiggrós, A. V. (2010). Vista de la hora de la soberaníaeducativa de AméricaLatina. https://revistas.udea.edu.co/index.php/revistaeyp/article/view/7727/7317

Pusterla, E. R. G. (2018). *Credibility of sovereignty—The political fiction of a concept*. Springer International Pu.

Rudiger, A. (2020). Pathways to education sovereignty: taking a stand for native children. *SSRN Electronic Journal*. https://doi.org/10.2139/ssrn.3877444

Seldon, A., & Abidoye, O. (2020). *The fourth education revolution was reconsidered: Will artificial intelligence enrich or diminish humanity?* The University of Buckingham Press.

Shengquan, Y., & Yu, L. (2021). *An introduction to artificial intelligence in education.* Springer Nature.

Tech Monitor. (2019, October 16). *Sovereign cloud: Where in the world is public sector data stored?* https://techmonitor.ai/technology/cloud/sovereign-cloud

The Artificial Intelligence Act. (2021, November 19). *What is the EU AI Act?* https://artificialintelligenceact.eu/

The Edvocate. (2018, August 16). *The dark side of educational technology.* https://www.theedadvocate.org/dark-side-educational-technology/

UNESCO (2021, January 26). *Stratégie Maroc Digital 2020.* https://en.unesco.org/creativity/policy-monitoring-platform/strategie-maroc-digital-2020

UNESCO. (n.d.). *Recommendation on the ethics of artificial intelligence.* https://unesdoc.unesco.org/ark:/48223/pf0000380455

United Nations. (n.d.). *Chapter I: Purposes and principles (articles 1–2).* https://www.un.org/en/about-us/un-charter/chapter-1

Université Mohammed VI Polytechnique. (n.d.). *The Moroccan international center for artificial intelligence.* https://www.um6p.ma/index.php/en/moroccan-international-center-artificial-intelligence

Yu, S. (2022). *Introduction to artificial intelligence in education.* Springer Singapore Pte. Limited.

Zemni, S., & Koenraad, K. (2006). *Morocco and the mirages of democracy and good governance - UCM*. (n.d.). https://www.ucm.es/data/cont/media/www/pag-72529/UNISCIZemni12.pdf

Chapter 9
Neurohacking and Artificial Intelligence in the Vulnerability of the Human Brain: Are We Facing a Threat?

Carlos Enrique Fernández-García, Dennis Vargas Marín, and Hernán Sotomayor Velásquez

Abstract The advancement of Artificial Intelligence allows the creation of high-impact experiences, focused on users. However, great dangers lie ahead in the fields of neuroscience and neurotechnology; as well as the computer, the human brain can be vulnerable to attack by hackers. This research offers a preliminary exploration of these thematic intersections that aim to know the state of the studies and present a discussion and a theoretical approach to the existing relationships between Artificial Intelligence and neurohacking in the teaching–learning processes. In this work, studies that address the symbiosis composed of Artificial Intelligence and brain hacking (neurohacking) as a process of manipulation and adulteration of the electrical activity of the brain are analyzed, at the time of restructuring the synapse processes. The results of our study reveal that neuroprogramming with Artificial Intelligence could, in the future, counteract bad neurohacking practices. It is concluded then that there is a growing interest in these disciplines that could be part of a global threat.

Keywords Neurohacking · Artificial intelligence · Processes · Brain hacking · Brain–computer interfaces

C. E. Fernández-García (✉) · D. V. Marín
National University of San Marcos, University City, Gate 3, Germán Amézaga, Lima, Peru
e-mail: carlosenrique.fernandez@unmsm.edu.pe

D. V. Marín
e-mail: dvargasm@unmsm.edu.pe

H. S. Velásquez
North Private University, Av. Guardia Peruana 890, Chorrillos, Peru
e-mail: hernan.sotomayor@upn.edu.pe

F. Roumate (ed.), *Artificial Intelligence in Higher Education and Scientific Research*, Bridging Human and Machine: Future Education with Intelligence,
https://doi.org/10.1007/978-981-19-8641-3_9

9.1 Introduction

9.1.1 Background

GIRI (2006) analyzes the scientific literature on Artificial Intelligence and its relationship with computer security. The post aims to alert us to the dangers of neurohacking in the future when bionic parts are becoming more common in humans. Cyborgs as a combination of human, mechanical, and electrical systems are on the lookout for neurohackers. The research, in its conclusion, contrasts the path traveled by informatics in the last decades that pass from the operation and repair of computer systems in the computer and that now are established in the human being.

Sokolovskaia and Volochkov (2021) argue that Artificial Intelligence is capable of exponentially improving the intellectual abilities of the average person. This superintelligence responds to new forms of effective thought for the preservation the advantages of the human brain in its competition with Artificial Intelligence. Trouble-hacker is one of those methods that seek to algorithmically solve a range of tasks. This literature review seeks to find the prototype of the person of the future who will base his superiority on artificial superintelligence.

Chattopadhyay et al. (2021) aim to develop in the consumer of intelligent products confidence in products with design such as social robots with Artificial Intelligence. The research aims to test the smart functionalities in these social robots to find potential flaws that violate IEEE principles. The results of the research show the vulnerabilities of the design of these social robots, in the event of an attack by neurohackers.

Astobiza et al. (2019) pose an ethical problem: How does the genuine intention of the user adhere to the signal that is processed and predicted by the brain–machine interface algorithm? The research aims to describe the classical theory of intentional agency and briefly explore algorithmic ethics in the context of brain–machine interfaces and how autonomy, responsibility, and data privacy are understood in this area. The research constitutes an ethical framework of principles that regulates neurotechnology and the new neuro-rights.

9.1.2 State of the Art

Artificial intelligence

Two million events occur at the synapse every second. The brain (hardware) is a computer, on which thoughts and identity (software) "run," whose programming is compatible with machines that perform complex functions after all and that allow us to speak, see, or think. Our brain processes information, encodes it, stores it, and retrieves it, just like a computer.

There are many similarities between the brain and the computer that we could describe as electrical neural networks and connectors. But what about the considerations of the possibility of endowing machines with "reasoning" similar to that of the human brain? Precisely, Turing (1950) is considered a pioneer in Artificial Intelligence by asking this question and establishing as an indicator of intelligence if a machine conversed with a human and did so naturally. Five years later, McCarthy et al. (1955) coined the term "Artificial Intelligence."

Since then, the technological and scientific advances of Artificial Intelligence and bioengineering, based on trial and error, today bear fruit and are about to change the course of evolution. Data mining, big data, data science, computer vision, and biotechnologies are concepts closely linked to Artificial Intelligence.

Artificial Intelligence is a complex field of computer science that is responsible for designing and building systems capable of simulating or imitating intellectual cognitive activities and states of the human mind by reproducing them in machines or making computers think. Bellman (1978) defines Artificial Intelligence as the automation of activities that we link with processes from human thought, activities such as decision-making, problem solving, and learning.

According to Sloman (1983), the subfields of Artificial Intelligence are circumscribed to sensory systems of perception such as artificial vision; robotics understood as the development of languages and tools, specific algorithms to perform some tasks; knowledge management, regarding the processing and interpretation of spoken and written language and of linguistic and non-linguistic multiagent systems; the architecture of affective and emotional mechanisms in intelligent autonomous systems; and learning and development techniques through evolutionary algorithms, problem solving, automatic designs, analysis of properties of different types of representations, techniques, and memory mechanisms.

Artificial Intelligence was initially oriented toward the development of algorithms for games, but its evolution includes automatic reasoning, the demonstration of theorems, expert systems, and language processing, referring to the behavior that the brain unconsciously assumes to perceive colors, and neural networks or connectionist systems that are computational models connected through artificial neurons to each other to transmit signals, among others.

The diversity of the applications of Artificial Intelligence has generated a range of possibilities of prescriptive procedures that have transformed the "rules in the software" of learning, by decisions based on probability functions derived from past experiences. The application of Artificial Intelligence is increasing in various industries worldwide and has a greater presence in developed countries such as Japan, the USA, and Asia. Benítez et al. (2014) argue that the most frequent applications of Artificial Intelligence are found in fields such as robotics, adaptive learning, image analysis, expert systems that allow data analysis and tasks, or automatic processing of texts.

Casado et al. (2021) argue that Artificial Intelligence systems use self-learning mechanisms that allow the development of projects and tools with which it is possible to interact with machines similarly to people do, with natural language and capacity training and learning.

Monasterio et al. (2019) define the algorithm as mathematical constructs that can use automated learning techniques, so they are not pre-programmed to make decisions based on sequential rules. The algorithm has a mind of its own, although a person writes it in such a way that he builds a machine, and then the machine changes by itself. Bazzara (2021) affirmed algorithmic automation in ultra-fast digital environments with continuous communication flows as a technological solution for social problems. Algorithmic designs build user profiles built from tracing past virtual movements, personalize content, and show great predictive capacity for future movements, tastes, and interests.

Cortés et al. (2021) focus on describing intelligent adaptive learning as an individualized model, highlighting methodologies and paradigms of Artificial Intelligence that determine a formative assessment, intelligent feedback, detailed explanations, routes adapted to the student's profile, and supports tutorials differentiated by levels.

Neurohacking

Artificial Intelligence systems are vulnerable to malicious use or neurohacking (Oliver, 2020). Brain hacking or neurohacking is defined as the manipulation of neural information or the increase in cognitive performance through the brain–computer interface (BCI) (Ienca & Haselager, 2016) or transcranial direct current stimulation (tDCS) (Wexler, 2017), a product of use or misuse of neurotechnology.

The brain is vulnerable to hacker attacks. This hacking is conceived as an attack on the human brain to extract sensitive data such as data and memories, including the ability to inject new information (Paganini, 2013).

In this regard, brain hackers study how to fool the human brain, be aware of its weak points, break its attention, and manipulate its consciousness. Martínez-Conde refers that magicians do not deceive us, but our brains.

Shujhat Khan (2019) argues that biohacking focuses on the brain and central nervous system to read or alter neural signaling to induce cognitive as therapeutic effects, psychological or adverse motors. This area is focused on modifying the electrical activity of the nervous system to improve physical and cognitive performance beyond traditional human limits.

Brain reading technology decodes and interprets mental states and processes, without directly accessing the functioning of the brain since it can establish a relationship between psychological processes and neural events (Mecacci & Haselager, 2019). Neurohacking techniques play a critical role in improving the central nervous system, since their overstimulation would affect specific regions of the brain and produce digestive problems, anxiety, and fatigue (Maslowski, 2016).

Wexler (2017) considers neurohacking as a branch of "life hacking" (or "quantified self"), a movement made up of people who program themselves to improve their performance. Neurohacking is intended to update the brain and enhance personal capabilities through the growth of new brain cells or also called neurogenesis.

Humans will be able to develop new senses or communicate directly with thought. Warwick (2019) argues that hacking the human body can have incredible applications, beyond the treatment of diseases. Humans will be able to develop new senses, communicate with multidimensional thinking, and have infallible memory, thanks to the technology implanted in their brains.

Yuste et al., (2017) warn that companies in trading data will even have referred information about what we think. Yuste is a spokesperson for 25 scientists who wish to incorporate five inalienable neuro-rights into human rights, such as mental privacy, personal identity, free will, equitable access, and non-discrimination (Molina, 2019).

Herranz (2017) classifies the types of hacking for ethical purposes as biohacking (the art and science of maximizing your biological potential), conscience hacking (explores the inner experience), flow hacking (the ability to experience programming where our creativity and productivity flow), and life hacking (neuroprogramming that introduces habits that are integrated into your lifestyle to achieve your goals).

There is little information in the scientific literature that links some of the effects of neurohacking in Artificial Intelligence systems. Ienca (2017) identifies three different types of neurohacking, outside of the malicious forms of neurohacking: input manipulation (type of brain hacking produced in the first phase of the brain–computer interface cycle); measurement manipulation (cyber-attack on the user during the measurement phase); and decoding and classifying manipulation.

General problem: How are Artificial Intelligence and neurohacking related to the vulnerability of the human brain?

9.1.3 Justification

Today, neurotechnology continues to cause a stir in all aspects of life; its transformative power leads us to face important challenges such as man–machine interfaces that allow us to extend the senses as a sensory toolbox to understand the environment or replace media. However, there is a direct impact on the risks related to biosafety issues and even their impact on these teaching–learning processes in a context of hybridization in technological advances in Artificial Intelligence.

The purpose of this compilation of sources is to publicize the reasons why the use and application of technology are justified from a social and business point of view in a given environment, but above all to understand the dangers of neurohacking.

The first reason is found in the educational environment. Today, various technological innovations present the creation of personalized educational systems that motivate learning in children and adults.

The second reason is the importance of its application in the business aspect, because thanks to the application of AI nowadays different business models have been created, which allow to shorten distances, reduce costs, increase productivity, improve processes, promote innovation, and be at the forefront of technology. This change in the labor market forces a professional re-education and the activation of creativity to be able to devise new business models that create new jobs and that allow you to lead a good lifestyle.

Finally, this compilation of citations from different authors shows different points of view and the relationship with the current environment so that you can have an idea of its risks, and advantages and consider its use and application in companies.

9.1.4 Hypothesis

The contributions of neurotechnology are providential to understand the teaching–learning processes in a context of hybridization in technological advances in the field of Artificial Intelligence and to answer the questions that arise, we propose the following starting hypothesis for new lines of research in the matter:

General Hypothesis. Artificial Intelligence positively counteracts the effects of neurohacking on the vulnerability of the human brain.

9.1.5 General Objective

To solve the problem posed in this research, the following objective has been proposed to know the state of the studies that analyzed the relationships between Artificial Intelligence and neurohacking in the vulnerability of the human brain.

9.1.6 Work Methodology

The methodology for this article is based on the scarce bibliography on Artificial Intelligence and neurohacking in Peru, to present a detailed analysis where the concepts, dimensions, and metrics are defined for an approach to this phenomenon applied to the processes of learning to teach.

9.1.7 Results

This section undertakes a review of the literature related to the different concepts, opinions, and criticisms of various authors, the concept and application of Artificial Intelligence and the effects of neurohacking in teaching processes are clearer. We have less and less control over who we are and what we believe in.

The Transnationals of Technology and Neurohacking

Artificial Intelligence already controls the world. Harari (2019) considers that large technology transnationals such as Google, Apple, and Facebook have years of investigating how to hack the human brain and use their techniques to shape the thoughts, feelings, and actions of their users, as occurs with sessions of cybertherapy with the use of Artificial Intelligence, the same ones that contribute to the improvement of mental health.

This type of "brain hacking" is a method capable of "destroying children's ability to concentrate" (Dalder, 2017). Neural circuits are activated in response to stimuli rapid responses that respond to stimuli that require deep processing.

This neuroprogramming is a way of hijacking people's minds to create a habit like when we wake up in the morning and the first thing, we do is check our social networks on our smartphones.

Social networks learn the chemical and electrical mechanism that regulates and defines the states of their users, through a very simple neuroscientific programming, built from six primary emotions: disgust, joy, rage, fear, anger, and surprise (Scaliter, 2017). The danger comes from the fact that these stimuli come from a mathematical equation executed by the ordinate and that they affect our feelings.

The hyperrealism of virtual reality in virtual simulators, for example, manages to hack the brains of its users, thanks to the Oculus Rift (Donoso, 2014).

Technology companies are capable of typing, in the brain, the buttons to activate cognitive tricks to amplify the results of their advertising strategies and "hack" the brains of the interlocutors, in full swing of technologies related to Artificial Intelligence and biotechnologies.

Koizumi et al. (2016) report that there are scientific studies that induce a slight memory of fear in the brain, associating it with an image, thanks to brief electric shocks. This neural "reprogramming" is associated with something positive rather than the feeling of fear.

Neurohacking and Mixed Realities

Neurohacking gathers data that leads us to create algorithms that lead them to click ads or links to sell us politicians and ideologies. If governments and companies succeed in hacking or hijacking the human operating system, they will be able to predict our decisions and manipulate our feelings. This is exactly what happens today with neuromarketing which is aimed at programming the wishes of consumers.

This "useful neurohacking" is a process of guidance of the nervous system, through internal and external stimuli, whose impact is evidenced in a didactic structure suitable for super learning. Video games convince the brain that any heat that is felt burns in the virtual environment.

The hyperrealism of 3D design motivates virtual roller coaster simulators to hack the brains of users of these video game technologies (Donoso, 2014). Even today, psychological disorders, particularly arachnophobia, are treated with visualization systems in acrophobic environments of augmented reality and virtual reality (Fernández, 2019).

Along the same lines, the Hirose Tanikawa Group has developed augmented reality systems to manipulate the user's feeling of having eaten enough, after changing the size of the meal (Ikinamo, 2012). On the other hand, a Peruvian company Feels Goods makes video games for the treatment of those who suffered strokes and cancer, to overcome the consequences that cause stress and anxiety (Fernández, 2017).

For their part, Ortiz-Catalan et al. (2014) investigate virtual reality or augmented reality treatments to relieve phantom limb pain with mirror therapy, which virtually reconstructs the amputated limb, generating an illusion of a restored limb in the brain, as inferred in the video (Neuromotus, 2014). It is also worth mentioning the impact of a South Korean documentary that shows the moments, where a woman interacts with the three-dimensional recreation of her daughter who was lost three years ago and who feels very real, thanks to virtual reality (El País, 2020). Technology is a double-edged sword. Vulnerability and totalitarian surveillance can become the force of the collective and visibility as a condition of all democracy.

Algorithms Grow in Intelligence

Users of this technology believe that the algorithm is designed to give them what they want, but it is not. The algorithm is looking for mazes that most closely match your interests to recommendation engines. Its evolution leads us to reflect on the importance of adaptation and learning in the use of algorithms.

Most of the schools in Peru today lack the knowledge of the advances in Artificial Intelligence in their daily management, since false information and rumors, the product of algorithms, are not fought.

Brain–Computer Interfaces

Neuralink, a company owned by Elon Musk, seeks to connect through neural implants that communicate with the human brain and computers. The idea of the brain–machine interface is similar to a neuronal cord composed of sensors and 3072 microscopic electrodes, which integrates a series of wires, throughout the brain, to restore capacities related to speaking, listening, or moving to people who have lost these capacities.

Regarding the use of EGG headbands, Caffo et al. (2018) argue the need to emphasize the development of statistical algorithms and signal processing that help in the process that takes raw images and the converted to those used for diagnosis or research.

With the implantation of electrodes in the motor cortex of the brain, an electroencephalogram is capable of interpreting or decoding the electrical records and executing what the nerve signals indicate. For their part, Steffen and Friedrich (2020) warn that direct manipulations of the affective states of people who are subjected to encephalogram readings are a major intervention in the mental configuration of a person, with potentially more lasting consequences that may include irreversible changes.

Eggs can detect "neural signatures" for potential threat detection. Helmets with binoculars alert soldiers to a danger that their brain subconsciously detects, allowing them to react faster.

Our brains will be fully unraveled and made technically accessible: Nanobots will fully immerse us in virtual reality and connect our brains neurally directly to the Internet, and we will expand our intellect by merging our biological brains with non-biological intelligence.

Angrick et al. (2019) develop a series of impressive advances in speech decoding using neural signals, duly mapped by EGG. High-quality speech has been reconstructed, during speech production, using deep neural networks.

The info neuronal united in symbiosis with the Artificial Intelligence of Neuralink will allow us to overcome, in short, the borders of the current human intelligence since the threads connected to the brain as a kind of "bandwidth." Konyshev is disappointed with the invasive neural interfaces designed by Elon Musk that require the challenges of complex surgery and rapid oxidation.

Brain–Machine Interfaces

Brain hacking takes over future scenarios, where the brain hacking interface and the manipulation of the algorithm that controls the technological device. We alert about warns about the perpetration of neuro crimes from the theft of brain recordings and the viability of remotely hacking these active medical devices that are vulnerable to electronic attacks and controlling robotic prostheses or blocking a brain implant.

Trends around scientific and technological developments in neuroscience, brain–machine interfaces, and forms of brain–machine interaction focus on the categories of human and machine, to turn us all, for sure, into cyborgs: humans and machines in a single being.

The term "cyborg" was coined by the American researchers, Clynes and Kline (1960), to highlight how the vulnerable human body could be technologically modified to meet the requirements of special exploration. The artificial parts are quickly included in the body scheme and felt as their "own."

The neurochip is a small device implanted in the human body that emulates the functioning of the synapse by allowing the interaction of the brain with a computer, based on brain–machine interfaces. Its speed is slower than that of the human brain, and its current use is for neuronal rehabilitation or supply of damaged or missing neurological functions.

Magan (2017) argues that electrical signals are released by placing a chip in the brain that allows for improving the symptoms of Parkinson's spinal cord pain, obesity of anorexia. "To advance in the study of the human brain is to discover the possibilities that would entail implanting electronic devices in it". What has not been done is the reading and writing of the neural code.

Researchers, at the University of California, discover how to translate brain images into English as a projection of a semantic space composed of maps of cortical planes.

Cyborgs are the product of biotechnological improvements such as neuroprostheses, artificial limbs, and exoskeletons that cross the border between humans and machines. Those prostheses integrate with the body through touch sensors. It incorporates them into the body scheme so that the brain recognizes the prosthesis as a natural part of the body. Neurohacking can even be done by intercepting signals that are transmitted over a wireless link from the brain to a computer or artificial limb.

The "neuroprostheses" or exoskeletons are an external structure that is used around the body to provide strength and power that the body does not possess, controlled in the future by thought. In the future, feedback may even be the product of feelings such as touch or temperature, based on multichannel stimulation of the cerebral cortex (Romero, 2006).

Warwick (2019) in Project Cyborg 2.0 discloses his project to become a cyborg, based on the experience of the development of implant technology, by inserting a set of microelectrodes under the joint, in a surgical intervention performed by Dr. Mark Gasson. Peter Kyberd used a neural interface so that Professor Warwick could control an electric wheelchair and an intelligent artificial hand.

9.2 Conclusions

Research on the harmful implications of AI neurohacking on society has blind spots. The great challenge for the university of the new millennium lies in the need to have intelligent educational tools of informatics that allow us to develop teaching–learning strategies, in addition to planning, designing, developing, and implementing digital skills, to train professionals capable of understanding and develop the technological environment, according to their needs.

It is worth mentioning that as an ally of learning, Artificial Intelligence must show positive neuroprogramming, with high biosafety, whose readings will be carried out with sophisticated machines that decode brain waves and that are part of the emotional information that we process unconsciously.

The application of Artificial Intelligence should be a key point in the discussions of significance concerning the new proposals in higher education, through the implementation of simulators, tutorials, or interactive game software with this adaptive technology to the rhythm and personalized needs of the students.

References

Angrick, M., Herff, C., Mugler, E., Tate, M. C., Slutzky, M., Krusienski, D. J., & Schultz, T. (2019). Speech synthesis from ECoG using densely connected 3D convolutional neural networks. *Journal of Neural Engineering, 16*(3). https://bit.ly/3tPeB3X

Astobiza, A., Ausín T., Toboso, M., Monte Ferrer, R.; Payá, M. A., & López, D. (2019). Translating thought into action: Brain-machine interfaces and the agency's ethical problem. *Journal of Bioethics and Law Bioethical Perspectives.* https://bit.ly/3sJpVNM

Bazzara, L. (2021). All the power to algorithms? Attendance, delegations, and modulations in the new governmental reason. *Arguments.* https://bit.ly/3nM61kh

Bellman, R. (1978). *An introduction to artificial intelligence: Can computers think?* Boyd & Fraser Pub. Co.

Benítez, R., Escudero, G. & Kanaan, S. (2014). *Advanced artificial intelligence.* Editorial UOC. https://bit.ly/3vyQIhC

Caffo, B., Zhao, Y., Eloyan, A., Wang, Z., Mejia, A., & y Lindquist, M. (2018). A survey of statistics in the neurological sciences with a focus on human neuroimaging. *En Wiley Stats*. https://doi.org/10.1002/9781118445112.stat08047

Casado, M., Mateos, M., Fermeso, A. M., & Sánchez, L. (2021). Impact of COVID on the education of people with intellectual disabilities. Use of chatbots as an innovative response based on the use of ICT. *Towards a Sustainable Research Model in Education*. https://bit.ly/3tgDnJk

Clynes, M., & Kline, N. (1960). Cyborgs and space. *Astronautics*. https://bit.ly/3oicdki

Cortés, E., Acuña, L. A., & Martínez, E. (2021). Covid-19 and intelligent adaptive learning in Higher Education: a literature review. https://bit.ly/3vEYVAZ

Chattopadhyay, A., Ali, A., & Thaxton, D. (2021). Assessing the alignment of social robots with trustworthy AI design guidelines: A preliminary research study. *11th ACM Conference on Data and Application Security and Privacy*. https://bit.ly/3eQ3vXt

Dalder, M. (2017). How Facebook 'hacks' your brain: they reveal the tricks that 'apps' use to provoke addiction. *RT*.https://bit.ly/3fKFQst

Donoso, E. (2014, April 28). The worst experience on a virtual roller coaster. [Video]. https://youtu.be/QPClWy7Pwl4

El País (2020, February 17). The VIRTUAL encounter of a mother with the AVATAR of her deceased daughter [Video]. https://youtu.be/NY-rGAmRyQo

Fernández, C. (2017, November 7). Neurohacking con realidad virtual [Video]. https://youtu.be/7WfV-TRf1mY

Fernández, C. (2019, September 25). Ticrauss [Video]. https://youtu.be/4jITH3NDXGA

Giri, B. N. (2006). Malware in men—Will you be protected? https://bit.ly/2QookQs

Harari, Y. N. (2019, January). The 'hacked' brains vote. *El País*. https://bit.ly/3wyYkC8

Herranz, A. (2017). Can your brain and your thoughts be hacked? *Innovation and Science*. https://bit.ly/3dMVEJz

Ienca, M. (2017). Hacking minds, hacking brains, hacking augmented bodies: Ethical aspects of Neurohacking. *The First Biannual Neuroadaptive Technology Conference*. https://bit.ly/3d9ZbBI

Ienca, M., & Haselager, P. (2016). Hacking the brain: brain-computer interface technology and the ethics of neurosecurity. *Ethics and Information Technology, 18*.https://doi.org/10.1007/s10676-016-9398-9

Ikinamo (2012, January 1). Change the size of food and your appetite with the AR system from Tokyo U [Video]. https://youtu.be/YftfOWT-0LM

Koizumi, H., Suehiro, E., Fujiyama, Y., Yoneda, H. Ishihara, H., Nomura, S. Fuji, M., & Suzuki, M. (2016). Effects of brain temperature on cerebrovascular autoregulation during the acute stage of severe traumatic brain injury. In B.T. Ang (Ed.), *Intracranial Pressure and Brain Monitoring XV. Acta Neurochirurgica Supplement*, Vol 122. Springer, Cham. https://doi.org/10.1007/978-3-319-22533-3_39

Magan, S. (2017). Is it possible to 'hack' the human brain? To be. Madrid, February 24, 2017. https://bit.ly/3tONuGq

Maslowski, C. (2016). Discovering neurohacking: The secret to a longer life. *How To Rewire Your Brain*. https://bit.ly/3scWUd8

Mecacci, G., & Haselager, P. (2019). Identifying criteria for the evaluation of the implications of brain reading for mental privacy. *Science and Engineering Ethics, 25*.https://doi.org/10.1007/s11948-017-0003-3

Molina, P. (2019, July). How scientists want to prevent your brain from being hacked. *BBC News World*. https://bbc.in/2Q0JDHl

Monasterio, A., Ausín, T., Toboso, M., Morte, R., Aparicio, M., y, & López, D. (2019). Translating thought into action: Brain-Machine interfaces and the agency's ethical problem. *Journal of Bioethics and Law Bioethical Perspectives*. https://scielo.isciii.es/pdf/bioetica/n46/1886-5887-bioetica-46-00029.pdf

Neuromotus. (2014, February 17). Phantom limb pain (PLP) treatment based on VR, AR, gaming, and MPR [Video]. https://youtu.be/0wp-SigTeLs

Oliver, N. (2020). Artificial Intelligence, naturally A manual of coexistence between humans and machines so that technology benefits us all. "*Thinking for the digital society*". *Number 1.* Editing and technical coordination National Observatory of Telecommunications and the Information Society. https://bit.ly/3nFyBE0

Ortiz-Catalan, M., Sander, N., Kristoffersen, M. B., Håkansson, B., & Brånemark, R. (2014, February 25). Treatment of phantom limb pain (PLP) based on augmented reality and gaming controlled by myoelectric pattern recognition: a case study of a Chronic PLP Patient. *Frontiers in Neuroscience, 8.* https://doi.org/10.3389/fnins.2014.00024

Paganini, P. (2013, 28 de August). Brain hacking, it's time to protect our mind from hackers. Ciber Defense. https://www.cyberdefensemagazine.com/brain-hacking-its-time-to-protect-our-mind-from-hackers/

Romero, S. (2006). Hardware/software environment for experimentation with visual neuroprostheses. [Doctoral thesis] https://bit.ly/3eQMZq0

Scaliter, J. (2017). When computers started controlling us. Remotely manipulated brain implants could alter our behavior. *La Razón.* https://bit.ly/3wYVfM3

Shujhat Khan, T. (2019). Transcending the brain: does it cost anything to hack into the nervous system? *Brain Communications, 1*(1). https://doi.org/10.1093/braincomms/fcz015

Sloman, A. (1983). Artificial intelligence. An illustrative overview. *The University of Sussex, Cognitive Studies Programme, School of Social Sciences, Falmer, Brighton BN1 9QN.* https://bit.ly/3vnlR7I

Sokolovskaia, I. E., Volochkov, I.V. (2021). The human needs of smart nations in the era of artificial intelligence. *Lecture Notes in Networks and Systems, 155.*

Steffen, S., & Friedrich, O. (2020). Wired emotions: ethical issues of affective brain-computer interfaces. *Science and Engineering Ethics, 26.* https://bit.ly/3nUKENS

Turing, A. M. (1950). Computing machinery and intelligence. *Mind a quarterly review of psychology and philosophy. Vol. LIX. Nº. 236.* https://bit.ly/3be78ED

Warwick, K. (2019). Project Cyborg 2.0. *Kevin Warwick.* https://bit.ly/2S1uq9T

Wexler, A. (2017). The social context of "do-it-yourself" brain stimulation: Neurohackers, biohackers, and Lifehacker. *Frontiers in Human Neuroscience.* https://doi.org/10.3389/fnhum.2017.00224

Yuste, R; Goering, S.; Aguera, B.; Bi, G.; Carmena, J.; Carter, A.; Fins, J. J.; Friesen, P.; Gallant, J.; Huggins, J. E.; Illes, J.; Kellmeyer, P.; Klein, E.; Marbleston, A.; Mitchell, C.; Parens, E.; Pham, M.; Rubel, A.; Sadato, N.; Sullivan, L.; Teicher, M.; Wasserman, D.; Wexler, A.; Whittaker, M.; y, Wolpaw, J. (2017). Four ethical priorities for neurotechnologies and AI. *Nature, 551*(7679). https://bit.ly/3dH0us6

Chapter 10
Ethics of Artificial Intelligence, Higher Education, and Scientific Research

Fatima Roumate

Abstract AI offers new opportunities to facilitate sustainable development and the inclusion of all actors within this process, which starts with education and science that were massively influenced by AI during the pandemic COVID-19 because of the transition of all countries to the hybrid system of higher education. This paper deals with the ethics of AI and scientific research. Three points are discussed in this paper. First, AI opportunities and challenges related to higher education and scientific research. The second is the importance of the ethics of AI in higher education and scientific research, and the third point is the new strategies and policy actions needed to ensure social development. As is concluded in this paper, optimal actions are needed, especially new international and national mechanisms, rethinking public policies, and reinforcement of the investment in this field becomes thus an obligation rather than a choice.

Keywords Artificial intelligence · Ethics · Higher education · Scientific research policy actions · Strategies

10.1 Introduction

The COVID-19 pandemic imposes new social and economic challenges, and it is facilitating the transition to a new era characterized by a large use of artificial intelligence (AI). These new tools are changing the world, and their impact on societies is unlimited. It is influencing all sectors and imposing new challenges on all actors (states, international organizations, NGOs, transnational corporations, and individuals). Nowadays, AI offers new opportunities to facilitate sustainable development and the inclusion of all actors within this process, which starts with education

F. Roumate (✉)
Faculty of Law, Economic and Social Sciences Agdal, University Mohammed V, Rabat, Morocco

Institut International de la Recherche Scientifique, Marrakech, Morocco
e-mail: iirs.institute@gmail.com

F. Roumate (ed.), *Artificial Intelligence in Higher Education and Scientific Research*, Bridging Human and Machine: Future Education with Intelligence,
https://doi.org/10.1007/978-981-19-8641-3_10

and science which are massively influenced by AI during the pandemic COVID-19 because of the transition of all countries to e-learning. The massive use of AI in education and science offers new opportunities such as ensuring qualified education for all and making scientific research easier. Therefore, it is also imposing new risks and challenges.

This chapter, therefore, attempts to examine AI implications on higher education and scientific research considering the importance of this sector and the race toward AI. The main questions one should ask are as follows:

Q1: How AI is changing science and how science will continue to surprise us with AI innovations?

Q2: What are the risks imposed by the malicious use of AI in higher education?

Q3: Could ethics in AI be a solution and help to create the universities we want in the future?

Q4: What are effective strategies and policy actions, which could address AI challenges imposed on scientific research and higher education?

To accomplish these objectives, the paper is divided into two sections. Section one analyzes the interaction between AI and science considering AI implications in higher education and scientific research with a special focus on malicious use of AI and how science will continue to surprise us with new AI innovations. In section two, the chapter draws on international mechanisms regarding the ethics of AI and new policy actions and strategies needed in this new era.

10.2 Interactions Between Artificial Intelligence and Scientific Research

Artificial intelligence (AI) is changing science considering its two pillars, which are higher education and scientific research. AI's impact on this sector is unlimited. This impact has been accelerated with COVID-19. New tools, apps, and technologies are now used in science and for future AI innovations. AI is at the same time the subject of study, scientific discipline, and tools. This leads us to another dimension of this complicated relationship between AI and science.

AI has a dual impact on higher education and scientific research. This duality is observed on both sides, which means that scientific research ensures the progress of AI innovations, and these tools are influencing scientific research and teaching. AI's positive impact on higher education and scientific research is significant. Malicious use of AI is imposing new risks on all users of AI technologies (Roumate, 2021a: 97).

10.2.1 AI Positive Implications in Higher Education and Scientific Research

AI is changing international society and societies. They are influencing all actors and sectors. These changes are significant and will be increased during the future decade.

Artificial intelligence moves universities and research centers to another stage in history with increased automation, digital performance, teleworking, e-learning, etc.

In this context, we cite the Charter of Human Rights and Principles on the Internet, which includes 10 principles of human rights in cyberspace; the first one is the right to access the Internet, as it enables everyone to have access to fundamental rights of freedom of expression, equality, education, etc. The question is how developing countries, in particular, can guarantee this right considered in the age of technological globalization as a prerequisite for ensuring the remaining fundamental rights of individuals, taking into account the number of individuals who has access to the Internet.

AI in education is growing from US$0.8 Billion to US$6.1 Billion in 2025. Augmented and virtual reality is expected to grow from US$1.8 Billion in 2018 to US$12.6 Billion (Bradley, 2021) (Fig. 10.1).

According to Yura Velichko, «The number of AR users is predicted to reach 4.3 Billion in 2025» (2022), this interactive technology will be the most important tool in higher education in the future considering its impact on this field for a practical learning, higher motivation and faster access to resources and knowledge. It has a role in improving distance learning throughout the inclusion of gamification in the learning process. Augmented reality will be more used in the future considering its access compared with VR, which requires special equipment like VR headsets and smart glasses (Velichko, 2022).

These technologies facilitate access to the international university considering learning, and this is exactly what the United States of America, in the mid-1990s, wanted to achieve when the World Trade Organization's Agreement on the Liberalization of Services considered e-learning a service sold and bought as a product. The worldwide situation with COVID-2019 has pushed states to choose e-learning as an

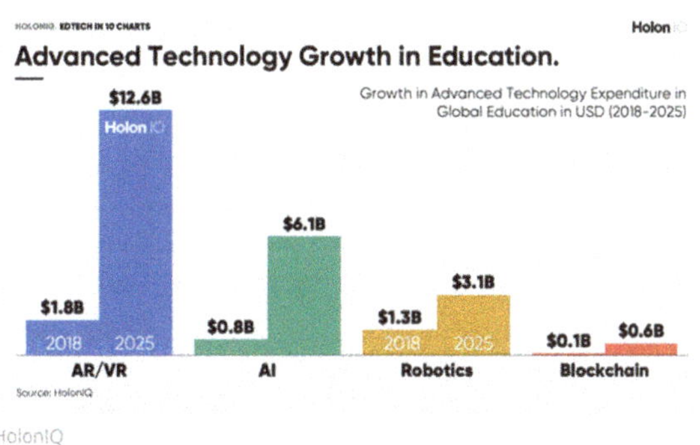

Fig. 10.1 Advanced technology growth in education, growth education in USD (2018–2025). *Source* Bradley (2021)

alternative and to rethink their education strategies to ensure the transition to a new education system characterized by the massive use of AI. Transnational corporations working in ICT are well prepared for this health crisis better than states because of their investments in AI and education during the last decade. Significant progress and innovations in machine learning and AI technologies are already experienced by teachers and learners in several countries. Therefore, significant challenges are also detected. AI ensures easy and free access to the information for teachers researchers and learners, but only if they have the Internet. AI ensures personalized education; therefore, transnational corporations are the leader in this field because they are investing more than some states.

Artificial intelligence also has implications for the labor market in general including the education sector, which is vulnerable to automation. A range of jobs will disappear, and new ones will be created. The new labor market will require a high level of education and new skills based on innovation and creativity. This will have a significant impact not only on the right to work or access to higher education but also on the right to human dignity, which is the main goal of all international mechanisms related to human rights. Overall, estimates range from 20 to 25 percent for current jobs at risk of disappearing in 2030 in each country, such as Northern Europe and Southeast Asia, while in Eastern European economies it will reach 40% (Mckinsey Global Institute, 2018: 1).

AI is creating important changes in the labor market due to automation which is changing jobs and skills. AI and 5G will «transform the nature of work and the workplace itself» (McKinsey Global Institute, 2018: 1). According to Jonathan Grudin, principal researcher for Microsoft, AI imposes three scenarios; the first one is that an important number of jobs will disappear in the future. The second scenario is that new jobs will appear, and the third scenario is that unemployed people, and they will need new policy actions to ensure human dignity (Smith & Anderson, 2014: 6). New policy actions are necessary also to face the malicious use of AI in higher education and scientific research.

10.2.2 Malicious Uses of AI, New Risks for Teachers and Students

In the era of AI, teacher–researchers and students are spending more time with machines and front of their laptops and phones, which means that they are more exposed to the risks created or enhanced by AI technologies considering malicious uses and abuses of AI. AI offers the possibility to analyze mass-collected data or human behaviors, moods, and beliefs based on available data and by manipulating videos (Bhatnagar & Cotton, 2018: p. 18). Sensitive information could be extracted during the learning process. Interaction between users (learners or researchers) and AI systems or machine learning offers the opportunity for malicious uses of AI such

Fig. 10.2 Global cybercrime damage costs. *Source* Morgan (2020)

as misappropriation or criminal exploitation of personal data including for marketing purposes during the research process and collecting knowledge.

AI tools facilitate access to scientific information to fight COVID-19. This means that state and non-state actors. Social networks are easy, and the various programs downloaded "free" from the App Store ensure easy access to data (scientific and personal and thus facilitate the search for each case of COVID-19 to mitigate the impact and magnitude of this pandemic. According to Steve Morgan, «global cyber-crime costs to grow by 15% per year over the next five years, reaching USD 10.5 trillion annually by 2025, up from USD 3 trillion in 2015. This represents the greatest transfer of economic wealth in history, risks the incentives for innovation and invest-ment, is exponentially larger than the damage inflicted from natural disasters in a year, and will be more profitable than the global trade of all major illegal drugs combined» (2020) (Fig. 10.2).

Before the pandemic, some universities suffered from cyber-attacks. In the United States, many universities have received cyber-attacks that increase daily, for example, The University of Delaware cyber-attack resulted in a data breach of approximately 72,000 current and past employees, including students. Other universities receive 90,000 to 100,000 attempts per day (Pérez-Peña, 2013). In the UK, 87% of universi-ties have received at least one cyber-attack according to VMware (2016: 5). For that universities are taking cyber-security to the top VMware (2016: 7), and they adopted several actions starting with the enhancement of the funding dedicated to cyber-security and training for security awareness considering technologies and practices. VMware's report suggests the creation of security-conscious culture, to think like a business and update its security strategy (2016: 7).

Since the beginning of the pandemic COVID-19, universities are increasingly targeted by cyber-attacks due to e-learning and because of the wealth of personally identifiable information and research data stored in their databases (Pitchkites, 2022). According to David Braue, «Ransomware will cost its victims more around $265 billion (USD) annually by 2031, Cyber-Security Ventures predicts, with a new attack (on a consumer or business) every 2 s as ransomware perpetrators progressively refine their malware payloads and related extortion activities» (2022). In higher education, ransomware attack costs $447,000 in 2020 (Morgan, 2020).

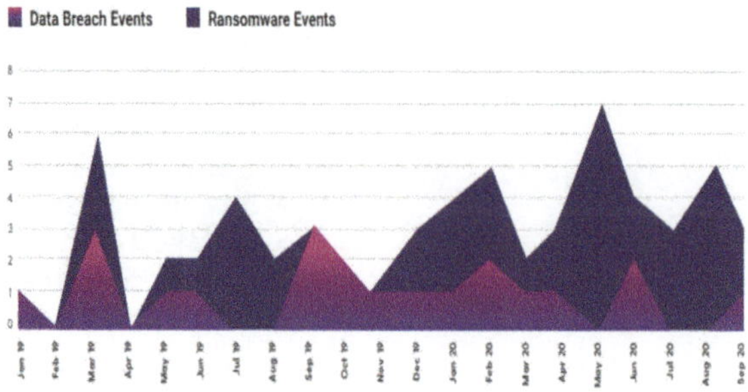

Fig. 10.3 Open-source cyber-events affecting higher education institutions globally. *Source* BLUEVOYANT: State of Education 2021 Report

Data breaches are also important sources of risk for higher education institutions which occupied half of the globally reported data breaches in 2019 (Morgan, 2020). Diagnostic shows that incidents are related to e-learning tools such as Zoom, Chegg, ProctorU, and other tools and login credentials or personally indefinable information (Morgan, 2020). «Over 200 universities have been impacted by a nation-state campaign since 2019». (Morgan, 2020). According to Brian Kelly, «In a poll of 154 institutions, more than 40% reported that security tasks have become much more important in the past year» (2021). Ransomware attacks against universities increased by 100% between 2019 and 2020 (BlueVoyant, 2021: 4) (Fig. 10.3).

Transnational corporations, especially high tech, updated their security strategies. Microsoft, for example, «released counterfeit, an open-source tool to help assess risk by allowing users to attack their own AI/ML» (Microsoft, 2021: 45). It also developed a responsible AI strategy in engineering (RAISE) initiative based on fairness, ethics, and transparency (Microsoft, 2021: 45). IBM has also established AI principles which are that the purpose of AI is to augment human intelligence, data, and insights belonging to their creator, and AI systems must be transparent and explainable (IBM Cloud Education, 2021).

Several high-tech companies elaborated AI principles and AI strategies to face biases, malicious use of AI including, cyber-criminality, and all negative implications of AI for today and the future. This leads us to the international instrument on ethics of AI and regional initiatives in this field.

10.3 Ethics of AI, New Policy Actions for Higher Education and Scientific Research

The ethics of AI is a new dilemma that urges international society to give a legal response to the ethical challenges created by AI. According to the AI ethics guidelines prepared by the AI HLEG, "AI ethics is a sub-field of applied ethics and technology and focuses on the ethical issues raised by the design, development, implementation, and use of AI. The goal of AI ethics is to identify how AI can advance or raise concerns about the good life of individuals, whether this is in terms of quality of life,

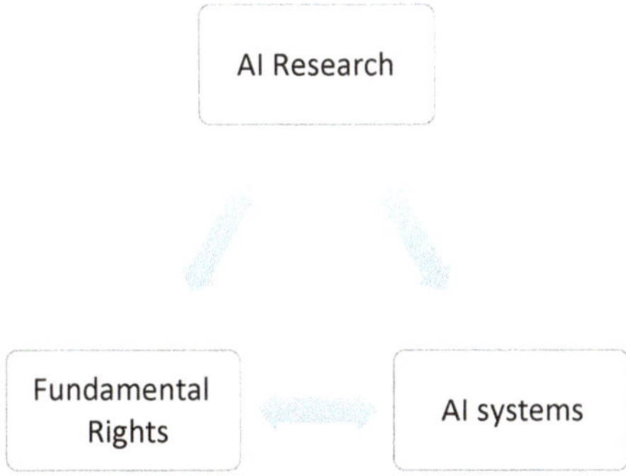

Fig. 10.4 Interactions between AI research, AI systems, and human rights. *Source* Made by the author

mental autonomy, or freedom to live in a democratic society" (AI HLEG, 2018: 9). Ethical purpose ensures compliance between algorithm and fundamental rights, and this compliance is based on Trustworthy AI (AI HLEG, 2018: 7) (Fig. 10.4).

In a sense, international society needs now, more than at any previous time, to consider the ethics of AI. Several intergovernmental organizations are focusing on this topic. New strategies are needed at different levels: international, regional, and national.

10.3.1 The International Instrument on Ethics of Artificial Intelligence

An international strategy on the ethics of AI aims to bring a solution to all challenges imposed by AI considering the gap between the Global North and the Global South. In this context, we underline the recommendation on the ethics in AI adopted by UNESCO in November 2021. Eleven policy areas set out in this international mechanism addressed to the Member States based on sovereignty and equality as it was included in international law. Even if the recommendation is not a banned document, it is the first instrument in this field, and it could guide international society in the AI governance process. Since November 2019, UNESCO has started to elaborate on the first global standard-setting instrument on the ethics of artificial intelligence in the form of a recommendation. For that reason, it nominated an ad hoc expert group (AHEG) composed of 24 individuals from different disciplines, representing all the regions in the world. The process includes inclusive and multidisciplinary consultations with a wide range of stakeholders. According to paragraph 104 of this recommendation, "Member States should encourage research initiatives on the responsible and ethical use of AI technologies in teaching, teacher training, and e-learning, among other issues, to enhance opportunities and mitigate the challenges and risks involved in this area." (UNESCO, 2022: 34). This recommendation underlines the importance of the right to research freedom, and it recommends several policy actions. According to paragraph 107, enhancement of public and private investment in AI research and ethics research is a real recognition that research contributes significantly to the further development and improvement of AI technologies. For that, it is necessary to create a bridge between academia and the private sectors to ensure the development of ethical AI (UNESCO, 2022: 35). Cooperation between academia and companies should focus also on the role of AI companies to ensure easy access to data considering relevant privacy and data protection standards (UNESCO, 2022: 35).

AI is revolutionizing scientific research, and for that, this recommendation underlines in paragraph 108, the importance of training AI researchers in research ethics to prepare them to «include ethical considerations in their designs, products, and publications, especially in the analyses of the datasets they use, how they are annotated, and the quality and scope of the results with possible applications.» (UNESCO, 2022: 35).

In this context, the enhancement between academia and legislative institution ensures the contribution of AI researchers to the elaboration of public policies (Fig. 10.5).

It is important to establish new mechanisms to facilitate scientific community participation to identify challenges and risks and to suggest new policy actions and strategies according to paragraph 111 of the recommendation (UNESCO, 2022: 35). Multi-stakeholders approach is considered also by some regional mechanisms related to the ethics of AI (Roumate, 2020: 144).

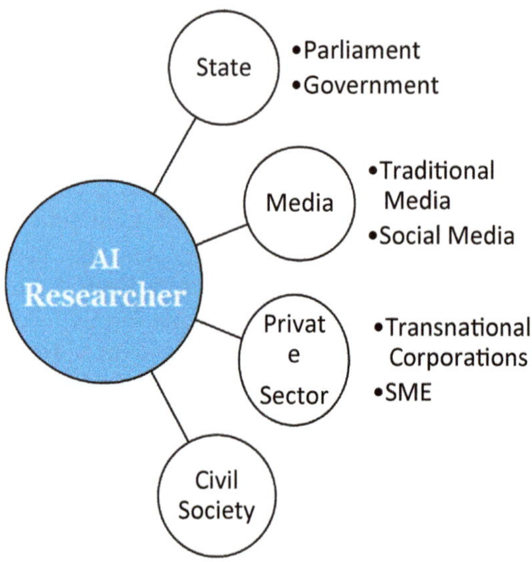

Fig. 10.5 Interaction between AI researchers and other actors. *Source* Made by the author

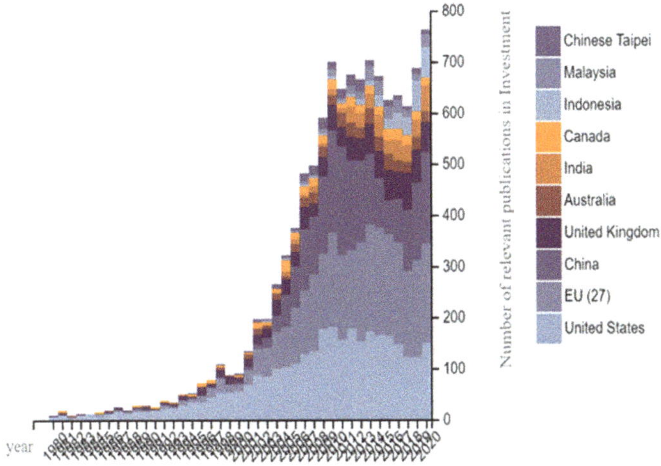

Fig. 10.6 Top countries investment—research publications. *Source* OECD AI (2022)

10.3.2 Regional Initiatives on the Ethic of Artificial Intelligence

The global debate on AI focuses on one of the most important issues which is technological and innovation sovereignty (Roumate, 2021b: 142). That explains the race to the investment in AI and the emergence of some good regional strategies to face AI challenges (Fig. 10.6).

United States is at the top with USD 45.000 Million, followed by China with USD 20.000 Million in venture capital investment and the EU with less than USD 5.000 Million (OECD AI, 2022) (Fig. 10.7).

In this context, OECD adopted a recommendation on AI on May 22, 2019. The OECD's recommendation identifies five value-based principles and human rights, well-being, democratic values, and respect for the rule of law are at the center of these principles (OECD, 2020a, 2020b). These values are based on the international legal framework, especially international human rights law.

This recommendation encourages investing in AI research and development both long-term public and private investment including interdisciplinary efforts. The goal according to Sect. 10.2 paragraph 2.1 line(a) of this recommendation is "to spur innovation in trustworthy AI that focuses on challenging technical issues and on AI-related social, legal, and ethical implications and policy issues." (OECD, 2019a). Public and private investment should focus also on open datasets that are representative and data protection to "support an environment for AI research and development that is free of inappropriate bias and to improve interoperability and use of standards" (OECD, 2019a). Therefore, the key question is the legal importance of this text considering that recommendations serve as non-binding guidelines, and international society needs an international instrument with powerful legal value.

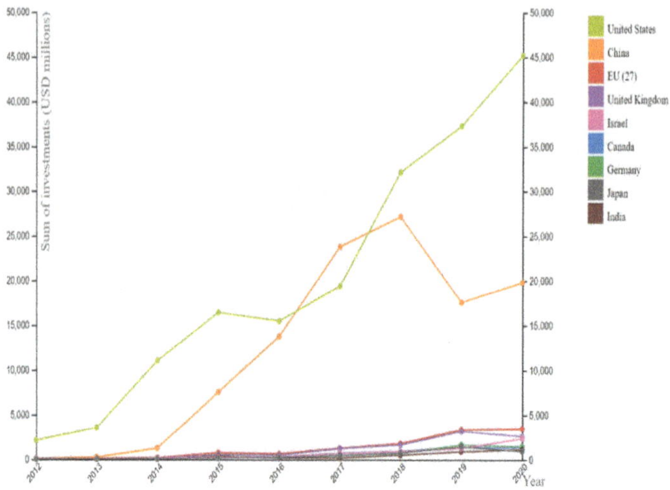

Fig. 10.7 Venture capital investments in AI by country. *Source* OECD AI (2022)

The OECD also implemented an AI Policy Observatory, which aims to offer the assistance needed by countries in enacting these principles and help them by encouraging, nurturing, and monitoring the responsible development of trustworthy AI systems for the benefit of society. Only, 40 countries have adopted these principles: 36 OECD member countries and six non-member countries (OECD, 2020a, 2020b).

In 2019, the Council of Europe created an Ad Hoc Committee on AI (CAHAI), which is working on "the feasibility and potential elements based on broad multi-stakeholder consultations, of a legal framework for the development, design, and application of artificial intelligence, based on Council of Europe's standards on human rights, democracy and the rule of law" (Council of Europe, 2019: 1). For this, the integration of AI in all scientific fields is crucial, and in this context, there are some weaknesses because AI research still limited to the STEM field as it is argued by OECD (Fig. 10.8).

After the pandemic COVID-19, AI is increasingly used in higher education and research due to the transition to the hybrid model. In medicine, for example, AI is increasingly used both in medical education and healthcare research (Georgiou et al., 2021). That is why the global artificial intelligence in healthcare market size realized an increase of 55.0% of AI healthcare market growth between 2020 and 2021 (Fig. 10.9), and it is expected to expand at a compound annual growth rate (CAGR) of 38.4% from 2022 to 2030 (Grand View Research, 2022).

AI research remains low in other scientific fields such as international law, political science, psychology, veterinary, nursing, dentistry, and other disciplines (Fig. 10.10).

The quality of AI research depends on the critical evaluation and proper monitoring of potential misuses or adverse effects meaning the importance of independent scientific research and the promotion of interdisciplinary AI research (UNESCO, 2022: 35). AI implications are extended to all sectors which is why AI research

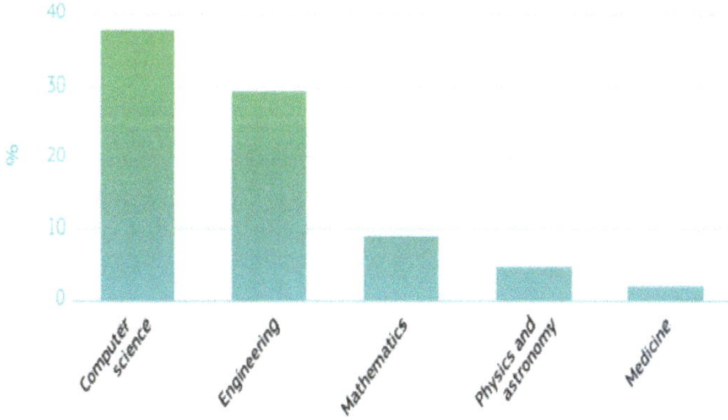

Fig. 10.8 Top 5 scientific fields for AI-related scientific documents as a percentage of all AI-related documents, 1996–2016. *Source* OECD (2019b)

Pandemic Impact	Post COVID Outlook
Artificial intelligence in the healthcare market grew at a rate of 167.1% from 2019 to 2021, in two years time-period.	The market is estimated to witness a year-on-year growth of ranged between 34.9% to 48.0% in the next 5 years
The pandemic supported the growth and development of AI-based technologies in healthcare and these technologies were widely being used in diagnosis, detection, claims settlement, patient management, clinical trials, and virtual assistants.	The growing shortage of care providers, the need to minimize the growing care expenses, the rising demand for value-based care, and the growing need to accurately and quickly diagnose and detect underlying health conditions to avail the optimum treatment plan at the earliest is boosting the adoption of AI technologies.
AI-based technologies were rapidly penetrating the healthcare industry and witnessed a significant surge in adoption in driving the quality of patient care and reducing the growing burden on the existing healthcare systems.	Market players are constantly devising product launches, technological collaborations, partnerships, and merger and acquisition strategies to expand their product portfolio and business footprint and sustain the tremendous growth trajectory of this industry.

Fig. 10.9 COVID-19, artificial Intelligence in healthcare market impact: An increase of 55% market growth between 2020 and 2021. *Source* Grand View Research (2022)

should be multidisciplinary not limited only to «… science, technology, engineering and mathematics (STEM)» (UNESCO, 2022: 35).

In a sense, several international organizations are working on rules and legal frameworks related to the ethics of AI, such as the European Commission's High-Level Expert Group on AI (AI HLEG, 2018), which elaborated the Draft Ethical Guidelines for Trustworthy AI. The goal of this initiative is to prepare European

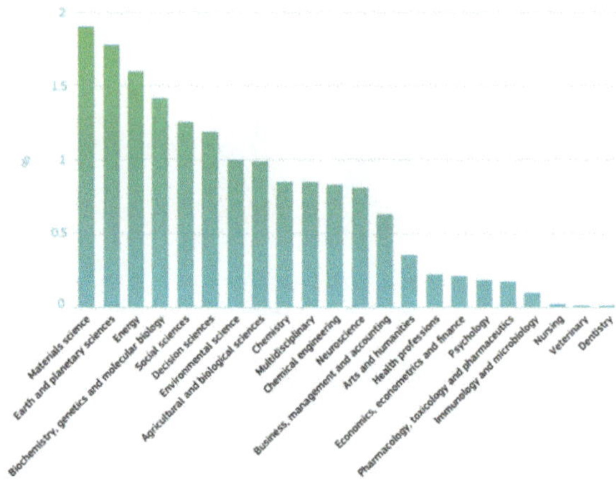

Fig. 10.10 Other scientific fields for AI-related scientific documents as a percentage of all AI-related documents, 1996–2016. *Source* OECD (2019c), measuring the digital transformation. *Note* Calculations based on Scopus Custom data, Elsevier, Version 1.2018, January 2019

countries for the tangible and intangible impact of artificial intelligence, including socioeconomic changes. Therefore, this goal is conditioned by respect for European values, which can only be ensured by an ethical and legal framework. Fundamental legal reforms and new policy actions are needed with the integration of all the stakeholders. The EU is based on a constitutional commitment to protect the fundamental and indivisible rights of human beings as cited in Articles 2 and 3 of the Treaty on the European Union and the Charter of Fundamental Rights of the European Union (European Union, 2017: 5). European Union also adopted several measures aimed to gain technological sovereignty, for example, the single European data market by 2030 (Valero, 2020).

Other regional instruments focus on the application of AI in a human-centered approach, for example, the G20 AI principles were adopted by the G20 Trade Ministers and Digital Economy in June 2019. The principles are drawn from the OECD recommendations on AI. The goal was to include a human-centric approach to AI, which is the only way to guarantee social development in the age of AI. According to these principles, trustworthiness in AI is at the center, and it needs the contribution of all stakeholders. Trustworthiness is the first principle cited because it is considered a cornerstone to ensuring social and sustainable development. As stated in the principles, "AI actors should respect the rule of law, human rights, and democratic values, throughout the AI system lifecycle. These include freedom, dignity and autonomy, privacy and data protection, non-discrimination and equality, diversity, fairness, social justice, and internationally recognized labor rights" (G20, 2019). In the same context, G7's adopted a Common Vision for the Future of AI in Charlevoix in June 2018 by the leaders of Canada, France, Germany, Italy, Japan, the United Kingdom, and the United States. It contains 12 commitments. This vision recognized that "AI that fosters economic growth, societal trust, gender equality, and inclusion depends on a predictable and stable policy environment that promotes innovation" (G7, 2018). Several actions are recommended to the state members based on "ethical and technologically neutral approaches" as was stated in the first commitment of this vision. According to this document, the leaders of G7 commit to «Promote investment in research and development in AI that generates public trust in new technologies, and encourage industry to invest in developing and deploying AI that supports economic growth and women's economic empowerment while addressing issues related to accountability, assurance, liability, security, safety, gender and other biases and potential misuse.» (G7, 2018: Para 2). The last example presented here is the African Union's (2019) Working Group on AI declaration as being adopted by African ministers responsible for communication and information and communication technologies (CICT) in Egypt on October 26, 2019 (African Union, 2019).

This important legal framework confirms that international society is convinced of the importance of ethics, which also means rules and strategic actions to face challenges imposed by AI, and the importance of updating international law in the age of AI.

AI technologies are growing faster than international laws (World Health Organization, 2020: 1). Thus, international laws need to be updated to consider all aspects of AI and its implications on social life, including automation, personhood, surveillance, and standardization. Burri argued that international law must be reviewed as AI entities possess legal personalities (Burri, 2017: 95). The proliferation of AI entities demands that international law reassesses this topic, but "neither international law nor will the work of international lawyers be automated because the data remains too limited for AI to learn to give a sound legal assessment"(Abhivardhan, 2018: 5). AI poses new challenges related to international law and international human rights law (Roumate, 2021c: 2). For that reason, there is a need to rethink international law and include ethical concerns in AI, which is the only way to ensure security and well-being.

The bridge between AI research and ethical values and principles related to AI needs to be integrated into national strategies based on the real coordination between academia, companies, and governments. National strategies on AI research and ethics mean strategic independence in different domains such as economy, society (education system, data privacy, human rights, culture, language, etc.), and policy, especially the protection of the democratic process from any foreign intervention using AI. AI infrastructure is a key to ensuring strategic independence, but also, it will facilitate the access of all social categories to human rights and knowledge in the age of AI to not leave anyone behind. This leads us to the governance of AI research and the importance of international cooperation in this field to reduce the divide between the Global North and the Global South.

10.4 Conclusion

In the era of AI, new reforms are needed at different levels considering the positive and negative implications of AI on higher education and scientific research and the interaction between these advanced technologies and this crucial sector. This interaction should be guided by the ethics of AI and ethics in science. For that new strategies on ethics of AI and higher education and scientific research are needed. International Corporations, especially high-tech and private sectors, are revolutionizing higher education and scientific research, but the impact of these changes and challenges or risks should be evaluated and monitored by states because guaranteeing human rights, peace, and security is the responsibility of a state.

If the result of AI research is, for example, lethal autonomous robots, states throughout international law and national legislation should bane this new type of arms to save humanity and ensure peace and security in all dimensions, for all. Governments should work with transnational corporations to build an enabling environment for data protection, transparency, and trustworthiness but more to make AI research at the service of humanity.

In the same context, international organizations should be, not only, a space of negotiation limited to the Member States, but it is time to create new tools which could facilitate all actors in the global governance of AI. National and international strategies need to be founded on three pillars: academia, companies, and governments. For that rethinking international law and national legislation is an obligation rather than a choice. In this sense, all fundamental notions linked to the state as a legal entity need to be reviewed, especially power and sovereignty considering the appearance of new types of sovereignty such as technological and innovation sovereignty. A new social contract needs to be established considering all social changes related to AI.

References

Abhivardhan. (2018). The Wider Realm to Artificial Intelligence in International Law. SSRN, 15 Mar. 2018. Retrieved from: www.papers.ssrn.com/sol3/papers.cfm?abstract_id=3172280

African Union. (2019). African digital transformation strategy, and African union communication and advocacy strategy among major AU initiatives in the final declaration of STCCICT3. Retrieved from: www.au.int/en/pressreleases/20191026/african-digital-transformation-strategy-and-african-union-communication-and

AI HELEG. (2018). Draft ethics guidelines for trustworthy AI. European commission's high-level expert group on AI. Retrieved from: https://ec.europa.eu/digital-single-market/en/news/draft-ethics-guidelines-trustworthy-ai

Bharnagar, S., & Cotton, T. (2018). The malicious use of Artificial Intelligence: Forecasting, prevention and mitigation, February 2018. Available at: www.eff.org/files/2018/02/20/malicious_ai_report_final.pdf

BlueVoyant. (2021). Cyber security in higher education. Retrieved from: https://www.bluevoyant.com/resources/cybersecurity-in-higher-education

Bradley, B. (2021). Global spending on virtual reality, AI in education poised to skyrocket, Report. Retrieved from: www.marketbrief.edweek.org/marketplace-k-12/global-spending-virtual-reality-ai-education-poised-skyrocket-report-says/

Braue. D. (2022). Global ransomware damage costs predicted to exceed $265 billion By 2031, June 2. Cybersecurity Ventures. Retrieved from: www.cybersecurityventures.com/global-ransomware-damage-costs-predicted-to-reach-250-billion-usd-by-2031/

Burri, T. (2017). International law and artificial intelligence. *German yearbook of international law 2017* (Vol. 60, pp. 91–108), Duncker & Humblot, Berlin, 2019. Retrieved from: SSRN: https://ssrn.com/abstract=3060191 or https://doi.org/10.2139/ssrn.3060191

Council of Europe. (2019). 1353rd meeting, Ad hoc Committee on Artificial Intelligence (CAHAI). Retrieved from: https://search.coe.int/cm/Pages/result_details.aspx?ObjectId=09000016809737a1

European Union. (2017). Consolidation version of the treaty on European Union. Official Journal of the European Union, C 326/17. Retrieved from: https://eur-lex.europa.eu/resource.html?uri=cellar:2bf140bf-a3f8-4ab2-b506fd71826e6da6.0023.02/DOC_1&format=PDF

G20 Insights. (2019). G20 AI principles. Retrieved from: https://www.g20-insights.org/wp-content/uploads/2019/07/G20-Japan-AI-Principles.pdf

G7. (2018). Charlevoix common vision for the future of artificial intelligence. Retrieved from http://www.g7.utoronto.ca/summit/2018charlevoix/ai-commitment.html

Georgiou Konstantinos, E. et al. (2021). 5G use in healthcare: The future is present. *Journal of the Society of Laparoscopic & Robotic Surgeons, 25*(4), e2021.00064. Retrieved from: www.ncbi.nlm.nih.gov/pmc/articles/PMC8764898/?msclkid=dbf2f95ebd1311ecb6eb77ddc2cc4adc

Grand View Research. (2022). Artificial intelligence in healthcare market size, share, and trends analysis report by component (software solutions, hardware, services), by application (virtual assistants, connected machines), by region, and segment forecasts, 2022–2030. Retrieved from: www.grandviewresearch.com/industry-analysis/artificial-intelligence-ai-healthcare-market

IBM Cloud Education. (2021). AI ethics. IBM, 13 March. Retrieved from: www.ibm.com/cloud/learn/ai-ethics#toc-ibms-point-CPxObWaf

Kelly. B. (2021). Cybersecurity in higher education: Going from 'no' to 'know'. EDSCOOP, May 26. Retrieved from: www.edscoop.com/cybersecurity-higher-education-brian-kelly/

McKinsey Global Institute. (2018). AI, Automation and the future of work: Ten things to solve for. Briefing note. Retrieved from: www.mckinsey.com/~/media/McKinsey/Featured%20Insights/Future%20of%20Organizations/AI%20automation%20and%20the%20future%20of%20work%20Ten%20things%20to%20solve%20for/MGI-Briefing-Note-AI-automation-and-the-future-of-work_June2018.pdf

Microsoft. (2021). Microsoft digital defense report, October. Retrieved from: http://query.prod.cms.rt.microsoft.com/cms/api/am/binary/RWMFIi

Morgan, S. (2020). Cybercrime to cost the world $10.5 trillion annually by 2025, special report: Cyberwarfare in the c-suite. Retrieved from: www.cybersecurityventures.com/hackerpocalypse-cybercrime-report-2016/

OECD. (2019a). Recommendation of the council on artificial intelligence. Retrieved from OECD/LEGAL/0449, https://legalinstruments.oecd.org/en/instruments/OECD-LEGAL-0449

OECD. (2019b). Measuring the digital transformation: A roadmap for the future. OECD Publishing. Retrieved from: https://doi.org/10.1787/9789264311992-en

OECD. (2019c). OECD principles on AI. Retrieved from: http://www.oecd.org/going-digital/ai/principles/

OECD. (2020a). OECD policy responses to coronavirus (COVID-19), using artificial intelligence to help combat COVID-19. Retrieved from: https://oecd.org/coronavirus/policy-responses/using-artificial-intelligence-to-help-combat-covid-19-ae4c5c21

OECD. (2020b). OECD AI policy observatory. Retrieved from: https://www.oecd.org/going-digital/ai/about-the-oecd-ai-policy-observatory.pdf

OECD.AI. (2022). Visualizations powered by JSI using data from Preqin. Accessed on 4/6/2022. Retrieved from: www.oecd.ai/en/dashboards/policy-areas/PA14

Pérez-Peña. (2013). Universities face a rising barrage of cyberattacks. NY Times, July 16. Retrieved January 21, 2015, http://www.upi.com/Top_News/US/2013/07/17/US-research-universities-increasingly-targeted-bycyberattacks/26641374065244

Pitchkites, M. (2022). Top cyber security statistics, facts & trends in 2022. Cloudwards. Retrieved from: www.cloudwards.net/cyber-security-statistics/

Research and Markets. (2022). Research and markets artificial intelligence in the healthcare market by offering (hardware, software, services), technology (machine learning, NLP, context-aware computing, computer vision), end-use application, end-user, and geography—Global forecast to 2025. Retrieved from: https://www.researchandmarkets.com/research/t3np23/artificial?w=12. Accessed March 29, 2022.

Roumate, F. (2020). Mechanisms of advanced international psychological security in the age of artificial intelligence. *Communications. Media. Design*, *5*(1), 143–156. Retrieved from: https://www.cmd-journal.hse.ru/article/view/11316

Roumate, F. (2021a). Malicious use of artificial intelligence, new challenges for diplomacy and international psychological security. In F. Roumate (Eds.), *Artificial intelligence and digital diplomacy*. Springer, Cham. https://doi.org/10.1007/978-3-030-68647-5_8

Roumate, F. (2021b). Ethics on AI and technological sovereignty. *Communications. Media. Design*, *6*(4), 139–151. Retrieved from https://cmd-journal.hse.ru/article/view/13766

Roumate, F. (2021c). Artificial intelligence, ethics and international human rights law. *International Review of Information Ethics, 29* (23/2021c). Retrieved from: www.crids.eu/cooperations/ethics-working-group-ifap/ifap_contributions/roumate_f_2021c-03_artificial-intelligence-ethics-and-international-human-rights-law.pdf

Smith, A., & Anderson, J. (2014). AI, Robotic and the future of jobs. Pew Research Center. Retrieved from: www.pewresearch.org/wp-content/uploads/sites/9/2014/08/Future-of-AI-Robotics-and-Jobs.pdf

UNESCO. (2022). Recommendation on the ethics of artificial intelligence. UNESCO Digital Library. Retrieved from: www.unesdoc.unesco.org/ark:/48223/pf0000381137

Valero, J. (2020). LEAK: Commission outlines a plan to create a single EU data space by 2030. Retrieved from: www.euractiv.com/section/digital/news/leak-commission-outlines-plan-to-create-single-eu-data-space-by-2030/

Velichko, Y. (2022). Using augmented reality in higher education: Benefits and challenges. Post Industri, January 27. www.postindustria.com/using-augmented-reality-in-higher-education-benefits-and-challenges/

VMware. (2016). University challenge: Cyber attacks in higher education. A Report. www.nextgensecurityforeducation.com/wp-content/uploads/VMWare-UK-University-Challenge-Cyber-Security.pdf

World Health Organization. (2020). Ethical considerations to guide the use of digital proximity tracking technologies for COVID-19 contact tracing. Retrieved from: https://www.who.int/publications/i/item/WHO-2019-nCoV-Ethics_Contact_tracing_apps-2020.1

Conclusion/Guidelines for the Future

This volume highlighted the interplay between artificial intelligence and higher education and scientific research, taking into account all the opportunities and challenges that could sometimes be scaled up in risks.

In addition, contributors suggested several recommendations that could guide all future actions associated with AI and its trends.

In a sense, artificial intelligence implies rethinking legislation and public policies, particularly higher education policy, considering the gap between countries and within countries in terms of AI and the importance of social cohesion.

To achieve this, a bridge between legislation and AI ethics is needed. This calls for a rethinking of the relationship between universities and the political environment and creates a connection between AI researchers and parliaments.

A multidisciplinary approach and the inclusion of multiple stakeholders in the development, implementation, and evaluation of such policy actions are crucial issues. However, the governance of AI should be state-led since guaranteeing human rights is the responsibility of a state and its ultimate goal according to the theory of the social contract.

Current global trends related to the digital transformation of higher education and hybrid universities call for stronger international cooperation than ever before. Bilateral and multilateral cooperation between the north and the south is a way to reconcile existing institutions and virtual universities. The race for technological and innovation sovereignty will enhance competition and cooperation among universities. This means that new strategies aimed at balancing competition and cooperation are more of an obligation than a choice.

In a sense, the scientific community should anticipate future challenges and risks and suggest solutions based on scientific reasoning as a cornerstone of a global strategic vision of higher education based on strong communication which could facilitate the inclusion of all stakeholders in the AI governance. That requires the

F. Roumate (ed.), *Artificial Intelligence in Higher Education and Scientific Research*, Bridging Human and Machine: Future Education with Intelligence,
https://doi.org/10.1007/978-981-19-8641-3

best knowledge of AI and the enhancement of ethical principles in everyday actions as a fundamental element to ensure technological sovereignty based on educational sovereignty.

Technological, innovation, and educational sovereignty should be a culmination point in all debates about AI governance. This requires a particular focus on how to reduce the neurohacking of AI and ensure a high level of protection against the malicious use of sophisticated machine learning that decodes brain waves.

For that, new strategies on the ethics of AI and higher education and scientific research are needed to develop human intelligence on a global scale based on ethical values since research on the ethics of AI could save human creativity and protect universal human values and principles.

www.ingramcontent.com/pod-product-compliance
Ingram Content Group UK Ltd.
Pitfield, Milton Keynes, MK11 3LW, UK
UKHW022210051026
15624UKWH00001B/90

9789811986406